# THE NORWEGIAN AMERICANS

# THE NORWEGIAN AMERICANS

James M. Cornelius

CHELSEA HOUSE PUBLISHERS

New York Philadelphia

On the cover: Women pose with their spinning wheels, Wisconsin, about 1873.

**Chelsea House Publishers**
Editor-in-Chief: Nancy Toff
Executive Editor: Remmel T. Nunn
Managing Editor: Karyn Gullen Browne
Copy Chief: Juliann Barbato
Picture Editor: Adrian G. Allen
Art Director: Maria Epes
Manufacturing Manager: Gerald Levine

**The Peoples of North America**
Senior Editor: Sam Tanenhaus

**Staff for THE NORWEGIAN AMERICANS**
Editorial Assistant: Theodore Keyes
Copy Editor: Terrance Dolan
Deputy Copy Chief: Ellen Scordato
Picture Research: PAR/NYC
Assistant Art Director: Laurie Jewell
Designer: Noreen M. Lamb
Layout: Louise Lippin
Production Coordinator: Joseph Romano
Cover Illustration: Paul Biniasz
Banner Design: Hrana L. Janto

First Printing

1  3  5  7  9  8  6  4  2

**Library of Congress Cataloging-in-Publication Data**
Cornelius, James, 1959-
  Norwegian Americans

  (The Peoples of North America)
  Bibliography: p.
  Includes index.
  1. Norwegian Americans—Juvenile literature.
I. Title.  II. Series.
E184.S2C67   1988      973'.043982      87-25613
ISBN 0-87754-892-7

# CONTENTS

Introduction: "A Nation of Nations"          7

Faring Well          13

The Northern Way          17

Vesterheim—The Western Home          31

The Boom Years, 1866–1914          49

Picture Essay: Celebrating the Heritage          65

Changing Allegiances          77

Making a Name in America          89

Passing the Torch          103

Further Reading          107

Index          108

# THE PEOPLES OF NORTH AMERICA

THE IMMIGRANT EXPERIENCE
ILLEGAL ALIENS
IMMIGRANTS WHO RETURNED HOME
THE AFRO-AMERICANS
THE AMERICAN INDIANS
THE AMISH
THE ARAB AMERICANS
THE ARMENIAN AMERICANS
THE BALTIC AMERICANS
THE BULGARIAN AMERICANS
THE CARPATHO-RUSYN
    AMERICANS
THE CENTRAL AMERICANS
THE CHINESE AMERICANS
THE CROATIAN AMERICANS
THE CUBAN AMERICANS
THE CZECH AMERICANS
THE DANISH AMERICANS
THE DOMINICAN AMERICANS
THE DUTCH AMERICANS
THE ENGLISH AMERICANS
THE FILIPINO AMERICANS
THE FRENCH AMERICANS
THE FRENCH CANADIANS
THE GERMAN AMERICANS
THE GREEK AMERICANS
THE HAITIAN AMERICANS

THE HUNGARIAN AMERICANS
THE IBERIAN AMERICANS
THE INDO-AMERICANS
THE INDO-CHINESE AMERICANS
THE IRANIAN AMERICANS
THE IRISH AMERICANS
THE ITALIAN AMERICANS
THE JAPANESE AMERICANS
THE JEWISH AMERICANS
THE KOREAN AMERICANS
THE MEXICAN AMERICANS
THE NORWEGIAN AMERICANS
THE PACIFIC ISLANDERS
THE PEOPLES OF THE ARCTIC
THE POLISH AMERICANS
THE PUERTO RICANS
THE ROMANIAN AMERICANS
THE RUSSIAN AMERICANS
THE SCOTCH-IRISH AMERICANS
THE SCOTTISH AMERICANS
THE SERBIAN AMERICANS
THE SLOVAK AMERICANS
THE SOUTH AMERICANS
THE SWEDISH AMERICANS
THE TURKISH AMERICANS
THE UKRAINIAN AMERICANS
THE WEST INDIAN AMERICANS

CHELSEA HOUSE PUBLISHERS

# A
# NATION
# OF
# NATIONS

Daniel Patrick Moynihan

The Constitution of the United States begins: "We the People of the United States . . ." Yet, as we know, the United States is not made up of a single group of people. It is made up of many peoples. Immigrants from Europe, Asia, Africa, and Central and South America settled in North America seeking a new life filled with opportunities unavailable in their homeland. Coming from many nations, they forged one nation and made it their own. More than 100 years ago, Walt Whitman expressed this perception of America as a melting pot: "Here is not merely a nation, but a teeming Nation of nations."

Although the ingenuity and acts of courage of these immigrants, our ancestors, shaped the North American way of life, we sometimes take their contributions for granted. This fine series, *The Peoples of North America*, examines the experiences and contributions of the immigrants and how these contributions determined the future of the United States and Canada.

Immigrants did not abandon their ethnic traditions when they reached the shores of North America. Each ethnic group had its own customs and traditions, and each brought different experiences, accomplishments, skills, values, styles of dress, and tastes in food that lingered long after its arrival. Yet this profusion of differences created a singularity, or bond, among the immigrants.

The United States and Canada are unusual in this respect. Whereas religious and ethnic differences have sparked intolerance throughout the rest of the world—from the 17th-century religious wars to the 19th-century nationalist movements in Europe to the near extermination of the Jewish people under Nazi Germany— North Americans have struggled to learn how to respect each other's differences and live in harmony.

Millions of immigrants from scores of homelands brought diversity to our continent. In a mass migration, some 12 million immigrants passed through the waiting rooms of New York's Ellis Island; thousands more came to the West Coast. At first, these immigrants were welcomed because labor was needed to meet the demands of the Industrial Age. Soon, however, the new immigrants faced the prejudice of earlier immigrants who saw them as a burden on the economy. Legislation was passed to limit immigration. The Chinese Exclusion Act of 1882 was among the first laws closing the doors to the promise of America. The Japanese were also effectively excluded by this law. In 1924, Congress set immigration quotas on a country-by-country basis.

Such prejudices might have triggered war, as they did in Europe, but North Americans chose negotiation and compromise, instead. This determination to resolve differences peacefully has been the hallmark of the peoples of North America.

The remarkable ability of Americans to live together as one people was seriously threatened by the issue of slavery. It was a symptom of growing intolerance in the world. Thousands of settlers from the British Isles had arrived in the colonies as indentured servants, agreeing to work for a specified number of years on farms or as apprentices in return for passage to America and room and board. When the first Africans arrived in the then-British colonies during the 17th century, some colonists thought that they too should be treated as indentured servants. Eventually, the question of whether the Africans should be viewed as indentured, like the English, or as slaves who could be owned for life, was considered in a Maryland court. The court's calamitous decree held that blacks were slaves bound to lifelong servitude, and so were their children.

America went through a time of moral examination and civil war before it finally freed African slaves and their descendants. The principle that all people are created equal had faced its greatest challenge and survived.

Yet the court ruling that set blacks apart from other races fanned flames of discrimination that burned long after slavery was abolished—and that still flicker today. The concept of racism had existed for centuries in countries throughout the world. For instance, when the Manchus conquered China in the 17th century, they decreed that Chinese and Manchus could not intermarry. To impress their superiority on the conquered Chinese, the Manchus ordered all Chinese men to wear their hair in a long braid called a queue.

By the 19th century, some intellectuals took up the banner of racism, citing Charles Darwin. Darwin's scientific studies hypothesized that highly evolved animals were dominant over other animals. Some advocates of this theory applied it to humans, asserting that certain races were more highly evolved than others and thus were superior.

This philosophy served as the basis for a new form of discrimination, not only against nonwhite people but also against various ethnic groups. Asians faced harsh discrimination and were depicted by popular 19th-century newspaper cartoonists as depraved, degenerate, and deficient in intelligence. When the Irish flooded American cities to escape the famine in Ireland, the cartoonists caricatured the typical "Paddy" (a common term for Irish immigrants) as an apelike creature with jutting jaw and sloping forehead.

By the 20th century, racism and ethnic prejudice had given rise to virulent theories of a Northern European master race. When Adolf Hitler came to power in Germany in 1933, he popularized the notion of Aryan supremacy. "Aryan," a term referring to the Indo-European races, was applied to so-called superior physical characteristics such as blond hair, blue eyes, and delicate facial features. Anyone with darker and heavier features was considered inferior. Buttressed by these theories, the German Nazi state from

1933 to 1945 set out to destroy European Jews, along with Poles, Russians, and other groups considered inferior. It nearly succeeded. Millions of these people were exterminated.

The tragedies brought on by ethnic and racial intolerance throughout the world demonstrate the importance of North America's efforts to create a society free of prejudice and inequality.

A relatively recent example of the New World's desire to resolve ethnic friction nonviolently is the solution the Canadians found to a conflict between two ethnic groups. A long-standing dispute as to whether Canadian culture was properly English or French resurfaced in the mid-1960s, dividing the peoples of the French-speaking Quebec Province from those of the English-speaking provinces. Relations grew tense, then bitter, then violent. The Royal Commission on Bilingualism and Biculturalism was established to study the growing crisis and to propose measures to ease the tensions. As a result of the commission's recommendations, all official documents and statements from the national government's capital at Ottawa are now issued in both French and English, and bilingual education is encouraged.

The year 1980 marked a coming of age for the United States's ethnic heritage. For the first time, the U.S. Census asked people about their ethnic background. Americans chose from more than 100 groups, including French Basque, Spanish Basque, French Canadian, Afro-American, Peruvian, Armenian, Chinese, and Japanese. The ethnic group with the largest response was English (49.6 million). More than 100 million Americans claimed ancestors from the British Isles, which includes England, Ireland, Wales, and Scotland. There were almost as many Germans (49.2 million) as English. The Irish-American population (40.2 million) was third, but the next largest ethnic group, the Afro-Americans, was a distant fourth (21 million). There was a sizable group of French ancestry (13 million), as well as of Italian (12 million). Poles, Dutch, Swedes, Norwegians, and Russians followed. These groups, and other smaller ones, represent the wondrous profusion of ethnic influences in North America.

Canada, too, has learned more about the diversity of its population. Studies conducted during the French/English conflict showed that Canadians were descended from Ukrainians, Germans, Italians, Chinese, Japanese, native Indians, and Eskimos, among others. Canada found it had no ethnic majority, although nearly half of its immigrant population had come from the British Isles. Canada, like the United States, is a land of immigrants for whom mutual tolerance is a matter of reason as well as principle.

The people of North America are the descendants of one of the greatest migrations in history. And that migration is not over. Koreans, Vietnamese, Nicaraguans, Cubans, and many others are heading for the shores of North America in large numbers. This mix of cultures shapes every aspect of our lives. To understand ourselves, we must know something about our diverse ethnic ancestry. Nothing so defines the North American nations as the motto on the Great Seal of the United States: *E Pluribus Unum*—Out of Many, One. ◆

*The Norse-American Centennial Parade drew crowds to downtown Minneapolis in 1925, marking 100 years of organized settlement in the New World.*

# FARING WELL

I n 1825, 52 Norwegians left Stavanger, Norway, bound for North America on the sloop *Restauration*. This voyage marked the first organized Norwegian emigration. As the 19th century progressed, thousands more Norwegians set out for North America. The numbers peaked at 29,000 in 1882, but the large wave continued steadily into the early 20th century. By 1925, the centennial of the *Restauration*'s landing, nearly 750,000 Norwegians had sailed to North America to make their new home in the United States or Canada.

Remarkably, the heavy emigration of the years 1865–1914, to which Norway lost nearly 25 percent of its population, paralleled the rise of a newborn spirit of nationalism in the Norwegian homeland. National pride could not make land more plentiful or more arable, however, and reports of expansive acreage in North America persuaded many to set sail for this wealth of opportunity.

Once they arrived, the immigrants transplanted the cherished customs of their homeland. As a result, Norwegian Americans tended to remain in their own communities, even after marrying and starting new families. Of the 3.4 million Americans today who claim Norwegian ancestry, more than a third of them claim solely Norwegian ancestry, though only 60,000 came over from the old country. Many of the remaining two-thirds who claim mixed ancestry have Swedish or Danish roots, giving them an entirely Scandinavian heritage. About 150,000 Canadians claim sole or partial Norwegian ancestry.

Today, Norwegian Americans rank among the most successfully assimilated groups of immigrants. They speak English, hold a variety of jobs in a diversity of fields, live comfortably among other Americans, and, most important, consider themselves Americans first and Norwegians or Scandinavians only by ancestry. In fact, Norwegians have become so completely assimilated into the American mainstream that we tend not to think of them as "ethnics." But they were considered foreigners when they arrived, and so suffered the prejudice of other Americans.

The 1980 U.S. census lists Norwegian ancestry as the 13th most common extraction in the land. (German ranks as the most common, then British; Swedish is 12th and Russian 14th.) In most regions of the country, the group constitutes a very small part of the population, except in the upper midwestern states, especially Minnesota, Wisconsin, and North Dakota—where more than half the people of Norwegian descent in America live.

As recently as 1945, an even higher percentage of the group lived in those states, but as America's overall population has shifted toward the West Coast, so have Norwegian Americans. Now almost one-third of them live in the western states. The states most heavily populated by Norwegian Americans include Minnesota (712,000), Wisconsin (392,000), California (368,000), Washington (286,000), and North Dakota (185,000). North Dakota has the highest percentage of Norwegian Americans in its state population with about 28 percent; in Minnesota, about 17 percent claim Norwegian ancestry.

These statistics reveal something unusual about Norwegians and their place in American society. From the time they first arrived in large numbers about 120 years ago, the Norwegians have chosen to live on the land or in small towns, and they continue to be the least urbanized of any ethnic group. Whereas almost 80 percent of all Americans now live in or near a city of at least moderate size, only about 60 percent of Norwegian Americans do. The same preference for rural and small-town life seems to prevail among Norwegian Canadians.

Norwegian immigrants had a reason for settling in rural communities: More than the citizens of any other nation, Norwegians came from farms and small villages in their native land, and therefore they gravitated toward similar surroundings in the New World. Many immigrants in America did not have as much say in the matter, especially the great wave of newcomers that arrived here in the late 19th century. Often displaced by war, religious persecution, or economic devastation, these refugees settled wherever they fit in best, usually in big cities on the East Coast or factory towns near the Great Lakes. Norwegian immigrants fared better. Permitted to congregate in smaller communities, often neighboring their former countrymen, they could preserve their culture and adapt to the new one at their own pace.

On the whole, Norwegian immigrants have been very successful in Canada and the United States, where they have enhanced food, architecture, language, politics, education, science, and sports. They have built a distinctive tradition of their own into American society, particularly in Minneapolis, Chicago, Portland, Seattle, Vancouver, and Brooklyn, the cities with the largest Norwegian-descended populations. They have also achieved a great deal in a multitude of smaller towns and rural sites in the upper Midwest. Their presence has fortified democratic institutions and added to the color of a heterogeneous landscape. Yet they have maintained their loyalty to the culture that created them. Their history in the New World represents, in the words of one historian, "a curious mixture of tradition and change." ❧

*More than any other ethnic group, Norwegians chose farming as their livelihood in North America.*

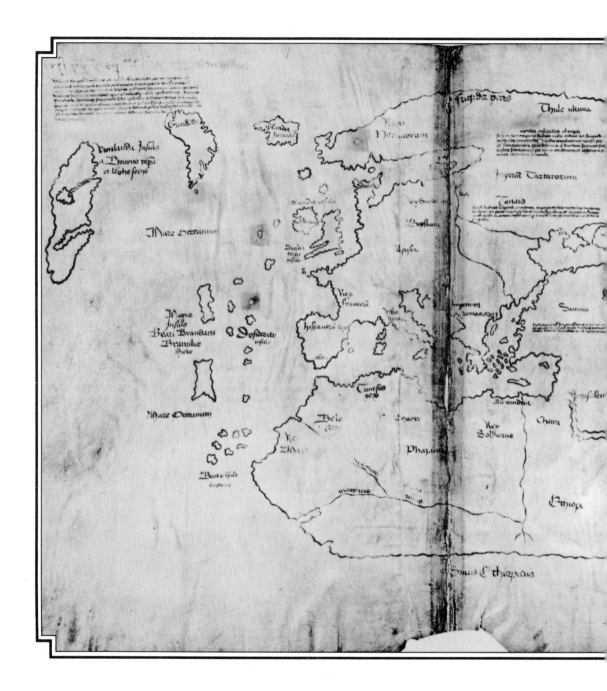

*In about A.D. 1000, 500 years before Columbus, Viking boatmen landed in North America. "The Vinland Map" depicts contemporary Greenland and part of Canada in the upper left.*

# THE NORTHERN WAY

The Kingdom of Norway, or *Norge*, which translates to "the Northern Way," is the smallest of the three nations that form the Scandinavian peninsula of northern Europe. The long border it shares with Sweden, its eastern neighbor, passes through the midst of a mountain range; in the far north it borders on Finland and the Soviet Union. Norway's shape resembles a large fish facing south, its tail flapping in the Arctic Ocean. The capital city, Oslo, commands the end of a large fjord (a narrow inlet of the sea) just where the fish's mouth would be. About half of the nation's 4.2 million people live along the Oslo Fjord. The next three largest cities, Bergen, Trondheim, and Stavanger, lie on fjords facing west toward the Atlantic. Norway stretches for 1,100 miles from north to south, occupying the same latitudes as Alaska, but because of its narrow shape from east to west, its land area equals only about half that of Texas.

Two-thirds of Norway's terrain is mountainous, the topsoil is thin and rocky, and lakes, rivers, glaciers, and forests cover much of the nation. Its rolling valleys and verdant countryside create a land that is extremely picturesque but difficult to farm. Only about three percent of Norway's land is arable, so farmers rely on dairying and breeding sheep, or on cultivating easily grown crops such as hay, oats, and barley.

*Norway occupies the western face of the Scandinavian peninsula. For centuries its people took to the sea as explorers and fishermen, but when the population boomed in the 19th century, they crossed the ocean to settle in the New World.*

Understandably, Norwegians have often relied on the sea for sustenance. Today three-quarters of the population live within 10 miles of the coast, working in the fishing, boatbuilding, and shipping industries. Perhaps because of this wide exposure to the sea, Norway has produced such noted seafarers and explorers as Roald Amundsen (the first man to reach the South Pole), Fridtjof Nansen (Nobel Peace Prize winner and Arctic explorer), and Thor Heyerdahl (an ethnologist who sailed from Peru to Polynesia's Tuamotu Islands on a balsa-wood raft, proving that the islands could have been settled by Indians from South America). Norway's earliest adventurers, though, and its first emigrants, were the Vikings.

## In Open Boats

The first documented Viking raid occurred in England in A.D. 793 and marked the beginning of an era in which Norse seafarers carved new kingdoms out of Europe's nations. The Vikings pirated as far south as the Mediterranean Sea and at one time controlled most of the North Atlantic, Great Britain, and the northwestern coast of Europe.

The most memorable Vikings were Erik the Red and his son Leif Eriksson. Erik the Red left Norway to settle Iceland, and in A.D. 985 he discovered Greenland. Eighteen years later his son, Leif Eriksson,

*Leif Eriksson, whose father, Erik the Red, discovered Greenland in A.D. 982, led transatlantic voyages in search of new territories farther south.*

reached North America in a long, open boat with about 30 oarsmen. Eriksson and his crew probably landed somewhere along the northeast coast between Cape Cod and Nova Scotia, though some historians believe they landed as far south as Long Island. The explorers found the new land to be plentiful in grapevines and other vegetation and decided to name it *Vinland.*

In Vinland the Vikings met redskinned men wearing animal furs, whom the Vikings dubbed *Skraelings,* or, roughly translated, "Fur-wearers." These Indians and Eskimos were peaceable and engaged in trade with the explorers, mostly bartering food for tools.

Many tales describe the journeys the Vikings made west, and although it is not certain whether they ever established a permanent settlement in North America, Norse boats did make it as far south as Hudson Bay, Canada. When the Viking era ended in about A.D.1100, the Norsemen had left behind legends and made discoveries important to the cultural history of Scandinavia and North America.

## The Coming of the Danish

Near the end of the 9th century A.D., before the time of Leif Eriksson, King Harald Fairhair unified Norway's petty kingdoms under his rule.

Harald's emergence as Norway's single ruler led many of the defeated rulers to join Viking expeditions, and Norway's merchant trade flourished through the 12th century. When Viking sea power waned, Norwegian merchants began losing ground to Germans and Russians. The country briefly prospered under the rule of Haakon IV (1217–63), but then fell under the political influence of outsiders, chiefly Denmark and Sweden. The telling blow came when the bubonic plague, the "Black Death," struck Norway in 1349, killing between half and two-thirds of the country's population and nearly destroying its dairy industry. Reduced to only a few thousand inhabitants by the late 14th cen-

*The prows of Viking ships were adorned with carved animal heads. A few have been preserved in museums.*

S non essent regiltrantes
et sutuis ministrantes que
viterut et que audiunt.
et illa que euemunt in diuersis
temporibus et in suis etrabus p
libros et per scripturas vbi po

que non viterunt nec saimt:
per scripturas edocemur
si nos bene recordemur. que sunt
bona vt amemus. quid ne malui
vt iutemus. Ergo tu scne co
dute ama scripturas. et stude.
et non amabis vitia. In auli?

tury, Norway was obliged to accept a royal union with
Denmark and Sweden, forming the Union of Kalmar
in 1397. Sweden soon broke from the union, but for
the next 400 years Denmark, Norway's southern neighbor across the Skagerrak Strait, greatly influenced the
Norwegian way of life.

Norway's culture soon reflected its close ties to Denmark. The traditional Norse tongue of ancient kings
and Viking mythology gave way to a Dano-Norwegian
mixture called *Riksmål* ("Official language"), which
was the medium of all legal and business activity. Most
country people, though, held onto their traditional lan-

*The plague, then known as the
Black Death, wiped out perhaps
half of Europe's population
during the 14th century and left
Norway with only a few
thousand people.*

*In the 16th century, Norway embraced the Protestant reforms of Martin Luther (shown here in a wood engraving). Lutheranism remains the nation's chief religion.*

guage. After Norway broke with Denmark in 1814, the use of Riksmäl faded as Norwegians began searching for a unified national language through which to assert their independence.

From the various regional dialects, poet and philologist Ivar Aasen (1813–96) created a distinctive Norwegian argot called *Landsmaal* ("Country language"). Aasen fought to have this speech of the commoners recognized equally with the Danish-oriented speech of the bourgeoisie. He wrote poems in Landsmaal describing peasant life, and for a while his crusade succeeded. But Landsmaal was not really anyone's mother tongue and inevitably gave way to a modernized version called *Nynorsk* ("New Norwegian"), spoken today by about 20 percent of the people, though that percentage is declining. Riksmäl, formerly the prevailing language of law, literature, and history, has also been modernized, into a less Danish tongue called *Bokmäl* ("Book language"), which is spoken by most Norwegians today.

## Under Danish and Swedish Rule

Until the beginning of the 11th century, Norwegians practiced a form of paganism centered around the worship of the Norse god Thor. In about 1020 Olaf Trygvason brought Roman Catholicism to Norway from England. The Catholic church held sway for over 500 years, controlling most political life as well as all religious activity. The church continued to own some of Norway's land until forced from the country in 1537, in the midst of Martin Luther's Reformation.

Luther, a German theologian, initiated a general protest in northern Europe against the dominance of and corruption within the Catholic church. Lutheranism removed some of the mastery of the priesthood from religious life, and its doctrine of protest (thus the term *Protestant*) caught on rapidly. The Danes embraced the Lutheran church and quickly made it the state religion of Norway as well. The Catholic church's lands fell to the government, which sold plots to individual citizens, thereby continuing Norway's reliance on smallholding (the farming of small plots of land) as the backbone of society. Almost all Norwegians adopted the new church, though today about 12 percent of the country observes other, mostly Protestant, credos, including Methodism and Baptism.

In Sweden, as in most of medieval Europe, the nobility imposed a harsh feudal system, forcing their own countrymen to work as serfs. But Norway did not suffer under such a harsh system. In fact, during the centuries of domination by Denmark, Norway came to have some control over its own affairs, though it was not yet master of its own destiny.

Although Norway had fallen under Denmark's sway, the more powerful nation was also dependent on Norway. During the European wars of the early 19th century, Norwegian soldiers were drafted to bolster the Danish army, which sided with the French emperor Napoleon. When Napoleon's power waned (he was finally vanquished by the English Duke of Wellington at Waterloo in 1815), Denmark was forced to give up its foreign possessions. Norway took advantage of the Danish losses and drew up its own constitution establishing a democratic monarchy. Christian Frederik was crowned as king. After a two-week war with Sweden, the monarch signed a treaty guaranteeing Norway's sovereignty within the Union of the Crowns, a partial union with the Swedes.

## Almost Free

The constitution was signed on May 17, 1814, at Eidsvoll, a town near Oslo that symbolizes Norway's democracy. *Syttende Mai*, or May 17, is still celebrated as Constitution Day to mark the end of Danish domination. The constitution lessened the powers of future kings and abolished the last two hereditary seats of the old aristocracy. One of the oldest democratic docu-

*This unusual 12th-century stave church is among Europe's oldest wooden structures. Christianity was a central part of life in Norway's towns and valleys, just as it would be for emigrants to America.*

*The* Storting, *the national parliament representing all classes since 1814, upholds the constitution that marked the end of Norway's union with Denmark.*

ments in the world, the Norwegian one drew inspiration from American, French, and Spanish models. One historian praises Norway at this juncture for being politically "far in advance of other European states." Under the Act of Union forged with Sweden, Norway had a great share in its own governing, and each country kept its own cabinet, armies, and customs.

Swedish rule proved less strict than the Danish had been, perhaps because mountains separated the two lands. More importantly, the Swedes did not seek the same degree of domination. Public sentiment in Sweden ran against the notion of forming an empire in the wake of Napoleon's imperial juggernaut. Norway also seemed prepared to uphold and defend the rights spelled out in its constitution. The Kingdom of Norway became its own master in 1905 when the union with Sweden was diplomatically dissolved.

The constitution set up a one-house parliament, the *Storting*, composed of men from all classes, and although women could not be elected to office, in 1907 Norwegian women became the first in Europe to gain voting rights. The main benefactors of this new order were the *bønder*, small-farm owners whose interests had previously been ignored by the city dwellers, high clergy, and Danish aristocrats. The bønder even managed to elect a majority to the Storting in 1833. Their leader, Ole Gabriel Ueland (1799–1870), has been compared to Abraham Lincoln as a reformist and defender of the disenfranchised. Ueland fought for the rights of the *husmen* (laborers who rented their land), the peasants, and the farmers, as well as for responsible spending by the governors.

The true spokesman for Norway's common people, however, was probably Henrik Wergeland (1808–45). A poet as well as a political thinker, Wergeland traveled throughout Europe to observe how societies had changed in the wake of revolutions in 1789 and 1830. He brought back to Norway new egalitarian and na-

*Haakon VII and Queen Maud became the first monarchs of a completely independent Norway in 1905, when the nation ended its union with Sweden.*

tionalist ideas, such as the belief that governments could, through growth and development, reflect more human values. In the political battles he waged and in his poetry, Wergeland was an irrepressible optimist, and his ideas and spirit spread throughout the country. Wergeland championed democracy in Norway as Walt Whitman celebrated the egalitarian spirit of America. His patriotic voice attracted the broad support that Norway's infant state needed to continue and improve. The era beginning in 1814, sometimes called the "Age of Wergeland," marked Norway's first step toward national unification.

## Education and Religion

Before the 19th century, education had been largely neglected in Norway's outlying districts, but as the century advanced, institutions of learning sprang up throughout the nation, increasing the Norwegians' rate of literacy and level of sophistication. In 1827 the first rural schools were established. Their main purpose was to ready children for religious confirmation at age 14. Students learned religion and reading for two or three months a year, but writing and math went untaught. Most youngsters in rural regions studied at home with the assistance of traveling schoolmasters of varying ability. However, in the mid-19th century a huge school-building effort began, and by 1890 literacy was nearly a nationwide achievement. Since then, Norway has been one of the world's leaders in the quality of education offered its citizens.

In the early 19th century, Lutheranism remained the official state church. Its leaders, most of whom came from the upper classes, trained in Denmark. These ministers, better off financially than their parishioners, became objects of envy. Parishioners felt further alienated by church corruption and by the rigid interpretation of the Bible favored by Norway's Lutheran theologians.

Then Hans Nielsen Hauge (1771–1824), a lay preacher and purifier, entered the scene. Hauge waged an antiauthoritarian campaign against the church and the political system, lending his name to the movement's title—Haugeanism. He felt that an individual's piety and belief in Christ mattered more than church law and that the clergy's intermediary position between God and the laity was an improper arrangement. By advocating more participation in the services for common worshipers, Hauge defied the established churches, which saw to it that he was imprisoned for seven years. Still, his influence ran deep. By the 1880s, laypeople had won the right to speak during the Lutheran service, a privilege they owed to Hauge.

Though most Norwegians maintained their Lutheran affiliation, some converted to other faiths. During the Napoleonic Wars, a few Norwegian prisoners were converted to Quakerism by Englishmen. These converts returned home to form a small but active group, thereby incurring the wrath of the government. The Quakers received fines for consecrating their births and deaths without sanction from the Lutheran church. At one point, 20 Quaker teenagers were jailed for their ignorance of the Lutheran catechism. Other groups sometimes ran afoul of the authorities, including Catholics and Jews. To all these people, and to dissenters from strict, high-church Lutheranism, the religious freedom of America looked particularly inviting.

## Causes Behind the Great Emigration

It is difficult to assess what affected Norwegians more: events in America, around Europe, or at home. Conditions at home probably had the greatest impact on the country's social temper, however. The average resident of Norway had little in common with the distant people of the new American nation, even though Norwegians admired America's apparent success in protecting civil liberties (for whites). Norwegians were similarly dis-

*Hans Hauge led a movement to allow the laity a greater role in church services. He was imprisoned for his activism, but Haugeanism became influential in both the homeland and Norwegian-American religious life.*

*Haymaking in about 1900. Norway's mountainous terrain made large-scale farming difficult and created a need for more land.*

tanced from the European culture that was thriving in the early part of the century as the Industrial Revolution began to influence urban development.

Until recently, scholars thought that most people moving around Europe between 1790 and 1920 were bound for the Americas. The new view, held by Harvard professor Bernard Bailyn, among others, is that a lot of the migration occurred *within* Europe. This argument holds true for Norway as well. Improved roads, education, and communications created opportunities away from the home village or farm. For example, as large commercial fishing fleets expanded, individual fishermen and their families were sometimes forced to move inland to look for work in the forests, mines, or farms. Oslo, a growing port city, attracted all kinds of people, from near and far. Railroads spread to the north, giving the isolated people there readier access to the rest of the continent. It was easier for men to pack up all their belongings and leave Norway than it was for women, and easier for young than old, but great numbers of both sexes and all ages soon set out alone.

Many migrated to the coast with the intention of emigrating west once they had saved enough money. But America was not alone in affording opportunities for those anxious to improve their station in life. A Norwegian had much to be thankful for in the native land: peace, a democratic constitution, a comparatively free religious life—three things known to few Europeans. Most Norwegians were also loyal to their native *bygd* (district), identifying with it and speaking the local dialect.

Good reasons for staying could not cure the land shortage, though—by 1907 the majority of farms were of less than 15 acres. This was hardly enough to sustain a large family, and an increasing number of younger sons who did not get their own parcel of land from the family farm were forced to move away. Meanwhile, scientific innovations reduced the need for some laborers. Industrialization came steadily after 1870 and threw many craftsmen out of jobs.

The population was rising dramatically, thanks in part to better medicine and to new crops, especially the potato, which became a staple crop after being introduced to Norway in the 18th century. During this time Norway's population rose an average of 1.7 percent each year, a figure that even accounts for the hundreds of thousands who left during the 19th century. What had been a country of 1 million in 1825 became a country of 2 million by 1900. And for a small nation covered with mountains, glaciers, and forests, the increase posed problems.

In the 20th century Norway has adapted quite well. Its rivers and fjords are harnessed for hydroelectric power; the nation's fine school system turns out many engineers and technicians; the discovery of oil and natural gas off the coast in the mid-1970s brought jobs and wealth; and the social-welfare system has virtually eliminated poverty.

The Norwegians of the 19th century faced a bleaker prospect. The union with Sweden stirred resentment among the many who wanted complete independence. The church acted slowly to accommodate the desire of some parishioners to speak their minds on the Sabbath. The rising population made the prospect of owning one's land a remote dream, and those who did own land felt the pinching competition from grain farmers in America, Canada, and Russia. North America seemed to hold the answer to all these problems. ⌇

*About one-quarter of Norway's population emigrated to the New World in the 19th and early 20th centuries, the second highest percentage (after Ireland) of any European nation.*

# VESTERHEIM — THE WESTERN HOME

Although many European nations had colonies in all parts of the world, by the beginning of the 19th century Norwegians had ventured only as far as Iceland and Greenland. But slowly the North American colonies began to attract Norwegians seeking land, adventure, or a religious haven. Though the larger chapters of the story of Norwegian immigration do not begin until 1825, a few pioneers made their presence felt in North America much earlier.

In 1620, the same year that the *Mayflower* landed at Plymouth Rock, a Dano-Norwegian expedition laid claim to land on the Hudson Strait in northern Canada. Six years later, a Norwegian sailor named Sand acted as interpreter for Peter Minuit when he bought Manhattan Island from the Canarsee Indians. A decade after that, a group of Norwegians settled in the Swedish colony in the Delaware River valley, while in upstate New York, Dutch landowner Jan Vanderbilt married a Norwegian woman, marking the beginning of one of the oldest and wealthiest families in the New World. In all, 57 Norwegians settled the colony of New Netherland (later New York State) between 1630 and 1674.

All in all, Norwegians did not figure significantly in the development of colonial America. Most arrived as sailors on board ships flying the Dutch flag and had little opportunity to transplant their own culture. Hans

*An artist's rendering of the sloop* Restauration, *which in 1825 brought 45 Quakers and 7 crewmen to New York. The event marked the beginning of large-scale emigration from Norway to the New World.*

Bergen, a ship's carpenter, became a major landowner in Brooklyn, New York, establishing a long-running community of Norwegians there, but for the most part colonial America was developed by peoples of the British Isles.

## Early Arrivals

The origins of sustained Norwegian life in the New World began with the sloop *Restauration*, which left Stavanger, Norway, on July 4, 1825, carrying 45 Quaker and Haugean pilgrims and a crew of 7. They became 46 while at sea with the birth of a child, and after a 14-week journey the travelers arrived at New York harbor on October 9. Captain Lars Olsen had hoped to sell his cargo of Swedish iron to recoup the cost of the boat ($1,400) and of the journey, but met with difficulties imposed by dockside authorities: The *Restauration* was impounded and Olsen fined $3,000 for carrying too many passengers. Eventually, news of the pilgrims' plight reached U.S. president John Quincy Adams, who waived the fine and issued a proclamation welcoming the Norwegians to America. Olsen sold the ship and cargo at a loss, but gained the immigrants' freedom.

The 53 steamed up the Hudson River to the newly opened Erie Canal, and across New York State to Kendall township, 35 miles northwest of Rochester, on Lake Ontario. Unfortunately, Kendall offered but poor soil for crops, and the rigors of chopping a settlement out of virgin wilderness led to the town's failure within 10 years.

The Kendall site had been chosen by one of the most colorful of all Norwegian Americans, Cleng Peerson (1783–1865). A native of Stavanger, Peerson knew many Norwegian Quakers and understood the persecution they faced, though he himself was not devout. In 1821, he left Norway to scout a new home for them. He saw potential in the area near the Erie Canal, which later fostered commerce and transportation by linking the Great Lakes with the Hudson River and hence New York's harbor. At Kendall, Peerson found a landlord willing to sell some of his property, but the Quakers wanted to farm, not to establish businesses, and for them the commercial potential did not compensate for the failures of the soil.

When Peerson realized the settlement could not attract others to Kendall, he set out on foot for Illinois. In 1834 he bought a parcel of land in what is now Ottawa, Illinois, by the Fox River, 75 miles southwest of Chicago, and waited for the rest to join him. Whereas the 40-acre tracts in New York cost $5 per acre, these went for just $1.25 per acre and the land was tillable. Peerson had visions of a canal connecting Lake Michi-

*This Norwegian postage stamp honored the trailblazer Cleng Peerson as a leader in the early settlement of New York, Illinois, and Texas.*

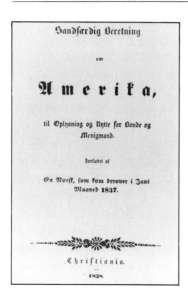

*Published in 1838, Ole Rynning's* True Account of America *was one of the first books to provide facts, not just rumors, about the hardships and rewards of emigration.*

gan with the Mississippi River, via the Fox River. No such canal was ever built, but with the later development of railroads, the town prospered anyway.

Peerson went on to found Norwegian settlements in Missouri, Iowa, and Bosque County, Texas, where he died at age 82. He returned to Norway three times to spread the word and to lead bands of newcomers across the Atlantic. Remembered as "half Daniel Boone and half . . . a new Moses," Peerson profited by his land speculation, but he worked hard for it. He stands as an eminent example of the wayfaring pioneer who opened up the American West.

After the early years of emigration, Norwegians grew more enthusiastic about prospects across the Atlantic, though some felt discouraged by the failure of Kendall. As conditions for the new Americans improved, they sent back letters published in Norway's newspapers. "We have gained more since our arrival here than I did during all the time I resided in Norway," one man wrote in 1835.

The excitement generated by rumors and dreams sometimes led to unrealistic expectations. As the bønder movement grew, however, Norway's farmers gained confidence, and those seriously interested in emigrating made plans. Help came from Ole Rynning, a curate's son who went to Illinois in 1837. His book *True Account of America*, published in Norway the next year, gave levelheaded reports on livestock, soil, education, language, and religion. Rynning recommended that travelers arrive in the New World by early summer, in order to plant buckwheat, turnips, and potatoes and to prepare for the long winter. America was the place to go for some people, Rynning advised, but it fell short of the paradise suggested by others. He even predicted that "bloody civil disputes" would arise over the question of slavery. When the entire town of Beaver Creek, Illinois, died of malaria, Rynning, only 34, among them, the tragedy provided proof of the difficulties in the new land. Still, his book ignited interest in life outside Norway, as did the families and religious groups who spread the excitement through word of mouth and shared reading.

By 1840 only about 400 Norwegians had immigrated to America, but by 1850 the number soared to about 15,000. This increase would be dwarfed by the huge groups that arrived after the Civil War, and for the most part these early immigrants remained isolated in Norwegian-speaking towns in distant Northwest America. At the same time, the great numbers of Irish fleeing the hardship of the potato famine and Germans escaping political turmoil overshadowed the population of Norwegians.

This surge of European immigration caused the price of a transatlantic ticket for the Liverpool-to-New York run to plummet from £12 to £3 in the years between 1815 and 1846. Though not all boats from Norway stopped in Liverpool, many did, and the larger ships, carrying more people, could lower the price and still make a profit on all runs. Lower fares encouraged even more people to sail.

*The 10-week voyage to the New World meant leaving behind possessions and loved ones, including family members too old to travel.*

Once a family decided to emigrate, preparations began in haste. Most people left in the spring and spent the preceding winter sewing warm clothes for the frigid American winter and building trunks to transport family heirlooms and essentials. As sturdy as they were ornamental, traditional Norwegian family trunks were reinforced by heavily wrought iron, and immigrants stuffed them with clothes, small personal treasures, household implements, and provisions for the voyage. In the new home, a trunk often served as table, chair, and closet until more items could be acquired. The farm wife and homesteader Gro Svendsen, who sent a remarkable series of letters from America to friends and family in Norway, advised women to sell every headdress, bodice, dress jacket, and kerchief, as there was no place in pioneer life for such luxuries. She also ad-

*The letters newcomers to America sent home were instrumental in spreading "emigration fever" among Norway's land-hungry farmers. This letter was mailed from Illinois in 1842.*

Til Agtbare Mand
Niels Olaisen Grime-
stad i Bergens Stift i
Norge.
To Bergen in Norvey.—

Jeffens Præri i Boon
County i Illinois Stat
den 1ᵉ Juni 1842.—

Kiære og uforglemme-
lige Moder, Datter og
Søster, og min kiære Ven
og Slægtning Isaach Olai-
sen Børke samt mine andre
Beslægtede og Velbekiendte

Venner, Jeg maa ikke for=
samme at tilbagesende Dem et
Skrivelse angaaende vores
Levemaade og Befindende,
siden vi Landede Lykkelig og
vel i Newyork Den 11ᵗᵉ August
1840. Den 13 Accoderede vi
Capitainen os Fragt til om
bord paa en Dampbaad for
13 Daler for Voksne Personer
og for vores Børn betalte jeg
intet og samme Dampbaad
trækkede 6 andre Baader efter
sig som de kalde for Svebaade.
Og til Albany kom vi den 15ᵈᵉ
sam: og i samme Stad blev vort
Tøi Veiet, og mit Tøi kom til en
Tyngde af 1100 Skaalepund og
huilket ieg havde at betale 6 Da

vised that women bring everything else they could fit, including a spinning wheel, because the quality of American goods was inferior to European products.

Ole Rynning's book advised passengers to bring enough firewood, water, and food to cook their own meals during the 12 weeks at sea. This meant tubs of butter and other commodities that inevitably spoiled before the 12 weeks were up. Another hardship for those cramped below decks, he explained, was that "passengers must furnish their own light." Rynning also recommended that rifles be brought along, for defense in the wilderness or for sale at a profit.

What immigrants did not pack they auctioned off. On the last day at the old home there might be a bon voyage party, though this festivity became less common once people began departing in droves. Immigrant groups traveled by sleigh or wagon to the coast (for many this was their first trip away from their hometown) and continued by sailboat to the larger ports, usually Stavanger or Bergen. There they could pick up last-minute articles or sell those items they had already tired of carting. Boarding the boat could be a shock: the crowding, the unsanitary conditions, regrets about leaving home, the fear of the unknown.

On board, immigrants enjoyed little diversion. In such close quarters, cooking was dangerous and difficult. The worst problem was rampant sickness; cholera, typhus (from lice), dysentery, smallpox, and measles took their toll. Gro Svendsen told of an infant's burial at sea: "It was all strangely quiet and solemn. The waves hurried to cover the little coffin." In 1842 the schooner *Ellida* docked in New York with 9 dead and 30 children requiring hospitalization. Soon afterward, the American and Canadian governments set up medical quarantine stations for new arrivals and eventually ordered the passenger lines to improve conditions. Finally, in 1863, the Norwegian government followed suit with enforced standards, but by then many of the Norwegian immigrants traveled aboard steamships sponsored by other nations.

*At first it was mainly individuals and the young who left for the New World, but by the mid-19th century whole families were making the trip.*

The passage was not unrelievedly bleak. A violinist often led singing after dinner, sometimes accompanied by a person playing a mouth harp or a small accordion. The passengers massed in steerage climbed up on deck for dances or just to stretch. Shipboard romances sometimes led to marriages performed by the captain, and most large ships witnessed the birth of a child somewhere between the continents. Children amused themselves by playing dress up, making rag dolls, or exploring what they could of their oceangoing magic carpet. And there was always the more serious diversion of trying to predict what would be found in the New World.

On arrival, one problem faced by newcomers was the dockside "sharper," a swindler who was eager to benefit from the newcomers' ignorance. Boardinghouse owners sent agents or "runners" to meet the ships and herd as many bewildered newcomers as they could into their shabby, overpriced hotels. Moneychangers took all the Norwegian *kröne* they could in exchange for a few dollars, and representatives of the railroads or inland boat lines hawked tickets to anyone who had not purchased one in advance. Whereas the process of emigration ended for many people when they disembarked in a large East Coast city, most Norwegians still had a long way to go. Before the Civil War, the journey often continued by boat through the Great Lakes, in some cases the conditions growing even worse than on the trip across the Atlantic. These journeys involved older boats commanded by less able captains, and the steerage-class passengers were packed in even tighter. One vessel sank in Lake Michigan, taking with it all on board. The journey made by wagon or train, though safer in some respects, often proved just as strenuous.

## Fanning Out

In 1836, a boatload of 200 Norwegians, the first since the *Restauration* 11 years earlier, set out for Fox River. These arrivals quickly spread out across northern Illi-

*"Runners" employed by boardinghouse owners would meet boats at the dock in an effort to fleece the unwary arrivals.*

nois, into southern Wisconsin by 1838, Iowa by 1839, Minnesota by 1851, and onward to the plains states of Nebraska and North and South Dakota. Permanent towns set up by Norwegian immigrants developed steadily in these few north-central states, though Texas, Missouri, and Utah also boasted small pockets of Norsemen. In fact, by the outbreak of the Civil War in 1861, Norwegian-born people lived in 32 of the 34 states, as well as in many of the western territories. Many had left Norway seeking land, and the Midwest had it in great store. From this point on, with the packing, sailing, and westward trek behind them, Norwegian Americans became among the most assimilated of any ethnic or national group.

Though the frontier had many great wonders in store, it also had a great many obstacles. Illinois had been admitted to the Union in 1819, but the great Sauk and Fox Indian chief Black Hawk controlled much of the state's wilderness until his defeat in 1832. Through the 1830s and 1840s, even without Indian attacks, the state that Norwegians spelled "Ellenaais" was still rugged and weather-beaten. At towns such as Fox River

*Before the Industrial Revolution brought machines to the midwestern farm, many settlers used only two oxen, a wagon, and a plow.*

The bounty of a typical
Wisconsin farm in the 1890s.

and Beaver Creek, gently rolling hills turned into prairie-flat expanse, harsh for people but ideal for wheat and vegetable gardening. The earliest houses, log shanties plopped down on a dirt floor, did not always provide adequate shelter. In winter the pioneers arose to find snow in their beds because of badly caulked log walls; in summer, flies pestered the animals and swarmed in the cabins. After two or three years of working hard and coping with such conditions, some families could afford to build a better house, away from the marshy, malarial sites they had learned to avoid. By 1850 Norwegian Americans made up 2,500 of the 81,000 Illinois residents; by 1860 the number rose to 6,000, and a decade later, 13,000. Some lived in Chicago, mostly sailors and their families, but most lived on the prairie.

In the late 1840s the center of Norwegian life in America shifted to Wisconsin and remained there for 30 years. The typical migrant came north from Illinois by horse or on foot to scout a piece of land. He then worked for wages on another man's farm until he could

*Most Norwegians came in search of land, and they found it in great supply on the American continent.*

purchase his own land, horses, and oxen, and move his family. The majority concentrated on wheat farming, but within a few decades they found success in dairying. Tobacco farming also caught on in a small way, and its introduction to Norway by a Wisconsin farmer exemplified how the two hemispheres learned from each other.

Northern Wisconsin is not farming country; its land is more suitable for lumber, mining, and fishing. Immigrants from eastern Norway tended to settle the southern part of the state, while those from Norway's coastal and timber regions headed for the forests and the shores of Lakes Michigan and Superior. In doing so, they transferred the differences in dialect and culture of the various Norwegian regions to Wisconsin in nearly unaltered form.

One of the more unusual communities of Norwegians was the Moravians, a small but influential sect of pietist Protestants who stressed Bible studies and personal religious experiences. In 1851 their pastor, A. M. Iverson, and an aristocrat named Nils Otto Tank, led the Moravians to Door County, the stunningly beautiful peninsula that juts into Lake Michigan northeast of Green Bay. The Moravians moved up north in an effort to separate themselves from their former, mostly Lutheran countrymen. At Door County they succeeded in building up the shipping and fishing industries, and lived in what some called splendor, thanks partially to Tank's funds. Today, Door County is a resort area as well, and many descendants of the original settlers remain.

At the start of the Civil War, 30,000 Norwegians lived in southern Wisconsin (most immigrants stopped first in Madison) and perhaps one-third that many resided in the north. The counties near the Illinois border were predominantly Norse, and Norwegians even outnumbered the French and Irish in Eau Claire. Lutherans composed the majority, having established their first church at Muskego, near Milwaukee, in 1839, and after that spreading Norwegian schools and newspapers throughout the state.

*Religious freedom attracted many immigrants. The Bible was central to the lives of most of them, in both rural and urban areas.*

In just a few decades, Norwegians from humble origins in Muskego—whose hotel was a converted barn—had come to own large, productive farms and good homes in town. Still, life was difficult: One letter writer in 1857 confided to friends back home, "Many people [who are] not adjusted to the climate break down." Not everyone had sunk their roots. Religious pilgrims moved on, trying to separate themselves from those Wisconsin churches still under the control of men trained in Oslo and loyal to the established Lutheran church. And land was still cheaper to the north and west, and its pull was strong.

Explorers forged onward to Minnesota Territory by 1850, leading the way for farmers. La Crosse, Wisconsin, proved the best place to cross the Mississippi River, and in the counties near it a group of 40 covered wagons set up a town. In 1870 half the Norwegian-American population still clustered in the counties near the Mississippi, such as Fillmore, Houston, and Goodhue, though the railroad began to provide easier dispersion across Minnesota.

This westward progression is illustrated well by the story of Steener Knutson and his family. In 1850 Knutson left Telemark, Norway, with his family. After landing in America they sailed through the Great Lakes to Milwaukee and rode by hay wagon to Dane County, Wisconsin, near Madison. The Knutsons farmed for 2

*Tobacco is still a valuable cash crop in parts of the Midwest. It was introduced in Norway by an immigrant who had farmed it in Wisconsin.*

years, then joined other families on a 14-wagon caravan to southeastern Minnesota. In 1869 the eldest son, Knute Steenerson (son of Steener), set off to look for cheap land by following the Sioux Indian trail northwest along the Minnesota River to a site near the South Dakota border. He was the first white settler in the region.

In the following years more Norwegians followed his trail to Sacred Heart township, and by this time Steenerson was able to sell them logs for houses. The 1870s, however, turned out to be the worst of times on the plains, with frequent droughts and grasshopper plagues; the local machine dealer was forced to reclaim the seeders and mowers from bankrupt farmers. When James J. Hill's Great Northern Railroad reached town in 1878, the community grew to include a saloon, two grain elevators, two hardware stores, a general store, board sidewalks, a hitching post, and new German and Irish neighbors. The Steenerson clan continued to do well, but what had begun as a Norwegian venture became, with progress, another melting-pot American town.

Norway's booming population and consequent land shortage sent a great number of have-nots, who aspired to own land and take part in free trade, to the New World. The idea of forming a colony of Norwegians led to the establishment of a few settlements. Hans Barlien, a former member of the Norwegian parliament, founded the town of Sugar Creek, Iowa, in 1839, attracting workers from Wisconsin's lead mines and other farmers barely eking out a living in Illinois. Barlien was frustrated because no self-sufficient colony of Norwegians had risen up in America, but of his own life in Iowa he wrote, "At last, I can breathe freely."

Iowa did indeed become an outpost of progress for Norwegians, though not the separatist or revolutionist place Barlien probably envisioned. Luther College at Decorah became the first American version of a Norwegian seminary, training young men for the clergy.

*Railroads and steamboat lines advertised open lands to immigrants and natives alike, singing the praises of towns that in some cases never materialized.*

In 1852, the great Norwegian violinist Ole Bull failed in his bid to start a Norwegian colony in Pennsylvania. This statue in downtown Minneapolis memorializes his effort.

Decorah was also home to the *Posten*, a leading Norwegian-American newspaper, and its literary offshoot *Symra*, which began in 1905. Decorah is now the site of Vesterheim, the museum of Norwegian-American heritage founded by Luther College in 1877.

## A New Country

*Vesterheim* translates as "Western home," an ideal not easily attained. Norwegians proved they could make the grade in the wilderness and adapt quite readily to new challenges, on their own or as part of a new, multinational civilization, but at least two communities intended to re-create Norwegian life in America failed quickly.

The first community, Oleana, Pennsylvania, was founded in 1852 by Ole Bull, a world-renowned violinist and folk hero in Europe and America, who was the subject of a poem by Henry Wadsworth Longfellow. Bull first came to America in 1843 and lived for five years in Cambridge, Massachusetts; Chicago; and Madison. During this time he developed the idea of establishing "a new Norway, consecrated to liberty, baptized with independence, and protected by the Union's mighty flag." He purchased 120,000 acres in Potter County, northern Pennsylvania, and settled there with about 250 other Norwegians, but his sympathies for the common people did not extend to a sense of what their "new Norway" should embody. Situated on hilly, forested terrain, Oleana proved impossible to farm (as had Kendall, New York) and within months all the residents moved to the Midwest to choose their own lands. Worse, Bull was defrauded by the co-owner of the property and became an object of ridicule. He returned to his musical calling in Europe, disheartened. Nonetheless, Bull is venerated today by Norwegian Americans for his experiment, and a statue of him stands in downtown Minneapolis.

The other short-lived Norwegian community began in Gaspé, Quebec, about 500 miles northeast of Quebec

City, on the Gulf of St. Lawrence. Not exactly a planned venture, Gaspé came into existence because docking fees were lower in Canada, and the human cargo could be replaced with Canadian timber for the voyage back to Norway. So most immigrant steamers between 1850 and 1870 called at Quebec before going on to New York. Those on board who couldn't afford the trip to New York or were too ill to continue stayed on in Quebec. The Canadian government appointed Christopher Kloster, brother of a Quaker leader, to promote Gaspé as a place with vacant land and nearby fishing. Kloster directed the destitute Norwegians to Gaspé and then returned to Stavanger to urge others to follow him back.

By this time, however, the authorities had apparently lost interest in the scheme. No town sprang up, the location proved farther from fishing waters than they had thought, and Kloster's lack of organizational ability doomed the town to failure in about two years. The 50 or so Norwegians who found themselves cut off and forgotten eventually left for America or the wilds of northern Canada.

For the tens of thousands of Norwegians who pushed west and chose to settle in locales of their own amid people of other nations, America delivered its promise. They quickly became part of the mainstream that would advance American social, cultural, and political institutions across the continent to the Pacific.

*By World War I, when scores of towns composed of Norwegian immigrants had been established in America, the group's political and cultural influence could be felt nationally.*

# THE BOOM YEARS, 1866–1914

Only a few thousand Norwegian immigrants arrived in the United States during the Civil War years, but in 1866 the number leapt to over 15,000. During the next 50 years, millions of Europeans crossed the Atlantic, constituting one of the greatest migrations in history. America's population surged from 36 million to 100 million by the start of World War I, and Norwegians added about 750,000 people to the commonwealth.

As a result of this great increase, the scale of Norwegian-American activities enlarged dramatically. More influential newspapers, churches, and schools appeared, and Norwegians began to gain a political voice locally and nationally. Though Norwegians had left their homeland in large numbers, they had left during an era of heightened nationalist sentiment, and many carried this strong sense of unity over to the Norwegian-American community.

## Norwegian-American Newspapers

The typical Norwegian newspaper in America began as a very small affair and often addressed a specific debate or audience. In 1847 Even Heg printed *Nordlyset*

(Northern Lights), the first Norwegian newspaper in America, in his cabin near Muskego, Wisconsin. The initial issue featured a Norwegian translation of the U.S. Constitution and some remarks by Representative Daniel Webster to the Congress. Later issues carried a translation of the Declaration of Independence and news of Norwegian-Americans' adventures during the California gold rush.

Minnesota's first Norwegian newspaper was published in 1857. The *Folkets Rost* (Voice of the People) printed its first issue on the eve of the local vote for statehood. In the same year the Illinois *Wossingen* began as a round-robin letter for natives of the Voss *bygd* (district) in Norway, bringing the transplanted Vossings news and gossip from afar. *Wossingen* survived in America for 14 years before moving back to Voss in 1871.

*The newspaper* Skandinaven *(1866–1940), founded by John Anderson, served Chicago's large Norwegian and Swedish community.*

The largest papers aimed at readers in the largest cities: *Skandinaven* in Chicago (1866–1940), also directed at the many Swedes there; *Minneapolis Tidende* (Minneapolis Times, 1887–1935), for many years the most influential; and *Nordisk Tidende* (Nordic Times, founded 1891) of Brooklyn, the only one of those three that still exists. *Nordisk Tidende* and the *Western Viking* (a sizeable weekly out of Seattle) have modernized, today printing about half the news in Norwegian and half in English.

Aside from news, some of the early Norwegian-language newspapers, including the *Decorah-Posten* of Iowa, ran literary supplements that served as breeding grounds for famous and aspiring writers. Thus, these Norwegian language newspapers served two purposes: to educate the readers in the ways of the new homeland and to keep them feeling connected to the old one. For example, *Emigranten* of Wisconsin, first edited by Danish Lutheran minister A. C. Clausen, printed an 80-part serialization of America's history and a shorter history of Wisconsin. He also ran, on the first page, the stories of Bjørnstjerne Bjørnson, Norway's most renowned writer. These publications also reprinted many items culled from newspapers in Norway, and likewise, the newswriters there did the same with notes from America, though this practice gradually faded.

Circulation never grew to more than a few thousand for any of the Norwegian-American gazettes, partly because few of their prospective readers had ever subscribed to a regular newspaper in Norway. The immigrants' reading habits changed along with their citizenship, however, and by the 1890s, 150 Scandinavian newspapers were circulating in America, the number continuing to grow until World War I, when speaking English became a badge of patriotism. When Bjørnson visited America in 1880, he expressed amazement that so many people read the newspapers, in any language.

## Standing Up for Freedom

Though disputes arose over many issues, such as land speculation, immigration by Catholics and Jews, and countless national political figures, nearly all Norwegians agreed about one question: the abolition of slavery. Before and during the Civil War, most of the Norwegian-American press portrayed slavery as an evil that did not belong in a Christian, democratic country. Some Norwegians disagreed, and a few periodicals controlled by tradition-minded ministers of the Norwegian Lutheran church, and particularly those published by the conservative Missouri Synod, a branch of the church, defended slavery. They argued that the Bible did not expressly forbid the owning of slaves as unchristian. The majority of letters to the press saw through this weak defense by noting that the entire spirit of the Bible opposed this restriction of human rights. Yet even after Lincoln had proclaimed the slaves free, the Missouri Synod would not denounce "the peculiar institution," causing A. C. Clausen to break from the synod in 1868.

Lincoln's legacy held most Norwegians, along with most northerners, in the Republican party until the end of the century, when new events altered the country's political climate. An economic panic in 1873 deterred many foreigners from seeking their fortunes here, but in 1882 Norwegian immigration peaked at 29,000 and remained almost that high each year until the economic collapse of 1893. (By comparison, almost 250,000 Germans entered American ports in 1882.) They remained concentrated in the country's prosperous farm belt, where most people blamed the setback on the railroad companies and Wall Street. Norwegian-American political loyalty began drifting away from the Republican party, which had thus far supported big business.

About half of all Norwegian Americans were farmers and another 10 percent worked as farmhands; a good many others were in some way dependent on the

farm economy, including Brooklyn sailors, Oregon lumbermen, and California ranchers and builders. In the early years of the 20th century, farmers and laborers began to speak up, just as Norway's peasant bønder had demanded to be heard a generation before. The movement away from the Republican party continued, and by 1920 about half of the Norwegian-American voting population switched over to the ranks of the Farmer-Labor party (which later merged with the Democratic party); others joined the Farmers Alliance or the Non-Partisan League, forces for progressive change.

These various expressions of activism, which were soon known collectively as the Progressive movement, called for improved conditions in the workplace, use of silver as well as gold conversion so that gold traders on Wall Street could not so drastically affect the economy, and public ownership of certain industries. Marcus Thrane, a socialist jailed in Norway for his part in the 1848 uprisings, led a Chicago crusade in the 1880s, demanding an 8-hour work day instead of the 10 or 12 hours then common.

*Political rallies were often held in rural regions in the 1870s and 1880s, when falling crop prices and rising land costs spelled doom for many an independent farmer.*

*Knute Nelson of Minnesota (at right), the first Norwegian-American senator, visited his birthplace in Voss, Norway, in 1898.*

Knute Nelson (1843–1923), a governor of Minnesota and later a U.S. senator for 30 years, also fought against the excesses of both business and labor. A Republican, he attracted support throughout the state by warning that "big cities may become dangerous monopolies, as [bad as] big railroads and big men." He helped enact legislation to ensure proper factory inspection and to get the railroads to assist farmers in marketing their crops.

The Pulitzer Prize–winning historian Richard Hofstadter points out that the era of agrarian unrest, capped by the Populist and Progressive movements, should not necessarily be seen as a reaction by farmers to the injustices forced upon them by railroads and big-money interests back East. Dissatisfaction may have arisen instead from the immigrants' failed hopes. For a Norwegian who had heard in letters about the vast wealth of America, and who then decided to try his hand at obtaining some of this new bounty, raising a moderately profitable harvest may not have been sufficient to offset his inflated expectations. And as land prices shot up throughout the Midwest and West, farmers may have had reason to fear for their future. Many farms changed hands, their old owners seeking greener pastures farther west or moving to the city for regular wages and greater social stimulation.

The reform wave that swept the upper Midwest in the 1890s and early 1900s had another cause, according to Hofstadter. He argues that the region's high foreign-born population did not arrive prepared for the frantic pace of American capitalism. Those newcomers were surely among the crowd who wanted the government to regulate the conditions that caused periodic upheaval in local economies and that created such poor working and housing conditions in the cities. Norwegians, accustomed to the more equitable division of national wealth in Norway, became a prominent force among those in America calling for policies that would generate more equal opportunities.

Meanwhile, the frontier continued expanding to the west. Illinois Norwegians who converted to Mormonism in the 1840s left for that church's new homeland in Utah. The discovery of gold in California in 1848 spread "gold fever" among thousands more. Mainly, though, the irrepressible American need to explore, wander, and stake out new claims, drew settlers to the mountains and beyond.

## Moving West

The Homestead Act of 1862 lit a fire under the westward movement. The act stipulated that any person 21 years of age or older who was a U.S. citizen or intended to become one could obtain title to 160 acres of land merely by living on it for 5 years, making improvements, and paying a $10 fee. As one historian put it, "Thus was the entire world invited to go west."

Pioneers went from Illinois to Iowa, from Dakota to Montana, Washington, and Alaska, clearing land and setting up homes. In 1862, the Sioux Nation rose up in violent response to the white man's rapid encroachment of its sacred lands, but with trains, dreams, greed, and rifles, the settlers pushed on and subdued the Indians by the 1880s. The discovery of gold in South Dakota, Alaska, and the Yukon Territory drew workers away from the volatile urban labor markets, and after the opening of the Panama Canal in 1913 many Norwegian sailors found work in the Pacific Coast ports. Norwegian contingents in Oakland and San Francisco, started in the 1870s, attracted more settlers.

In 1896 the Canadian government passed a bill of its own designed to attract farmers to the vast northern

*The Homestead Act of 1862 encouraged the quick and inexpensive sale of virgin lands (often through the railroad companies) to anyone willing to cultivate them. Hundreds of thousands of Norwegians answered the call over the next 60 years.*

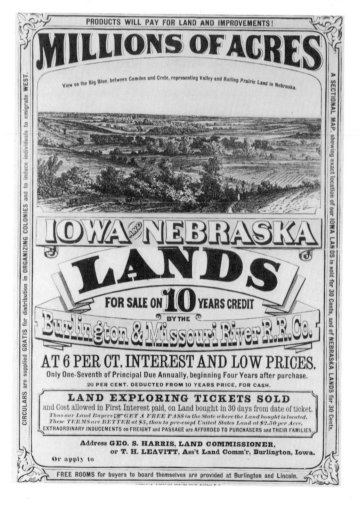

prairies. Recruiters went to the Red River Valley of Minnesota and to North Dakota to encourage families to emigrate across the border. Scandinavian Americans made up a high percentage of those who took the offer, and many Norwegians moved to the farm towns in the provinces of Alberta and Saskatchewan, as well as to coastal sites in British Columbia. But the exodus never reached more than a few hundred before the Canadian government dropped the unsuccessful policy in 1911. Too many open lands lay in the less harsh climate south of the border.

The westerly push brought some individual Norwegians to prominence. Anton Holter came from Norway as a child, then worked as a gold prospector, farmer, factory owner, silver trader, and lumberman, living in six different western states. Later he introduced streetcars to Montana. Martha Ostenso moved with her family to Winnipeg, Manitoba, and in 1925 won a major literary prize for her novel (written in Norwegian) *Wild Geese*.

These few led remarkable lives, but for most the immediate rewards of settling the West were less grand. One of the most fabled Norwegian Americans, Snowshoe Thompson (born Jon Toreson), for 20 years carried a 75-pound mail sack through a 90-mile mountain pass wearing oak-slat skis. Clearing land to farm in Washington State meant chopping down or burning trees of 30-foot diameter. Herding reindeer in Alaska (brought from Lapland, northern Norway) was also taxing. New fishing fleets or salmon canneries in Seattle, Vancouver, or Juneau sometimes did not show a profit for years.

Norwegians in the Pacific Northwest found a landscape similar to that of Oslo or Bergen, and many chose to settle near the water. The new opportunities in fishing, building, and shipping encouraged migration from the plains by landless younger sons and by Norwegians

*Folk hero Snowshoe Thompson, newly arrived from Norway, carried the mail through mountain passes in California and Nevada for 20 years.*

*Some farmers spent whole winters logging the north woods. And many Norwegians in the Pacific Northwest made forestry their full-time livelihood.*

recently thrown out of work by the mechanization of their crafts or by the demise of sailing ships. In addition, farming in the West was not necessarily the perilous, one-crop venture it could be in the Midwest. A farm family could keep busy all year producing hops, fruits, and berries, and maintain a sheep ranch at the same time.

Merchants and businessmen also found easier entry into trade in the West, because customers did not turn away at the sound of a foreign accent as they did in the old cities of Minneapolis, Madison, or Chicago, where native-born Americans dominated commerce. Ethnicity blurred in the West, especially in California, where in many cases the Norwegians, Swedes, and Danes would join in one Scandinavian society. By 1900 about 50,000 Norwegians lived in Washington, and 20,000 in Oregon; by comparison, 250,000 called Minnesota home, and the percentage involved in Norwegian churches and clubs was much higher in the Midwest than in the West.

Though the South was never a Norwegian stronghold, some headed there. Johannes Nordboe left Kendall, New York, in 1841 with his wife and 3 sons to farm near what is now Dallas, preparing the way for a community that included 5,500 Norwegians by 1930. Comanche and Kiowa Indian raids took their toll on the settlement, and fire and illness also beleaguered the Texans. Johannes Reierson, the Texans' unofficial leader, composed a guidebook that bolstered settlement and morale. He wrote, "A new spirit is awakened in these immigrants, a feeling of independence and freedom, a spirit of tolerance in matters of religion." Other information about 19th-century Texas came from Elise Waerenskjold, a prolific letter writer, teacher, and

*Their seagoing history prepared Norwegian Americans for the fishing industry along Washington's Puget Sound.*

leader in the temperance movement. (Alcoholism was a serious problem in rural areas.) One local custom she recorded was the "fencing bee," a gathering at which people collectively sharpened sticks and tied them with wire, making fences for the cattle. In treeless parts settlers built rock walls and, using only hammers, chisels, and saws, quarried stone for houses.

Most Norwegian Texans owned slaves before the Civil War, though very few fought in the Confederate Army. Some even went north to join the largely Norwegian 15th Wisconsin Regiment. After the Civil War, the victorious Union government began offering southern lands at no cost to migrating northerners. These giveaways, combined with the balmier climate, lured some midwestern Norwegians south to the farms of Vir-

*The town of Norse, Texas, and the surrounding region became home to a few thousand Norwegians beginning in the 1850s.*

ginia. Still, only a few hundred Norwegians settled south of the Mason-Dixon Line, and a woman in Tennessee summed up their sentiments when she wrote a friend up north that she felt "cut off."

## Developing Cities and Railroads

The capitals of Norwegian-American life continued to be Minneapolis and Chicago, the respective headquarters of the milling and railroad industries. In Minneapolis, Norwegians founded and inhabited entire sections of the city, creating a welcoming community for their compatriots.

The life of John Honmyhr illustrates the story of many a Norwegian immigrant in Minneapolis. In 1881, at age 19, Honmyhr left Norway and his family behind, and soon got a job at the Washburn Crosby flour mill (now General Mills). He lived near the mill, near the Mississippi River, until he could buy a house in a new neighborhood four miles to the south, from where he walked to work. He married a Norwegian-American woman and settled in the same neighborhood, where his countrymen owned most of the shops, and the Lutheran minister lived around the corner. His citizenship papers said he would "renounce forever all allegiance and fidelity to any foreign Prince, Potentate . . . and particularly to the King of Sweden and Norway whereof he is a subject." Until the 1980s some of his great-grandchildren lived in that same neighborhood, the majority of their ancestry still Norwegian.

Though Minneapolis claims a higher percentage of people of Norwegian ancestry, Chicago boasts a greater number of Norwegian Americans. The Chicagoans tended to be skilled craftsmen who built houses just beyond the downtown area until the next wave of immigrants, consisting of Poles, Italians, and Czechs, came along. At first, Norwegian Americans tried to retain their ethnic community, but they soon dispersed to all parts of the city and suburbs.

*Laying the tracks and manning the depots, Norwegian Americans helped extend the transcontinental railroad from the Dakotas to the Pacific Coast in the 1870s.*

In the late 19th century the transcontinental railroad provided unprecedented mobility. In 1882 alone, trains carried almost 800,000 Europeans across the North American continent, including about 100,000 Scandinavians. The railroads fostered great employment possibilities, quickening expansion of the frontier. In fact, by providing loans, special passenger rates, and demonstrations of new farm machinery, the railroad companies were able to sell six times the acreage that the government did under the Homestead Act.

In North Dakota there arose a phenomenon called the "bonanza farm," in which railroad companies such as the Great Northern purchased huge plots of land and hired hundreds of workers to produce tons of wheat.

Though hardly a democratic way of distributing the land, the bonanza farms did provide work for the thousands of Norwegians and others who arrived with only muscle and stamina. Knut Hamsun, a Norwegian novelist who won the Nobel Prize for literature in 1920, worked one of the bonanzas in 1887, and described it this way:

> The prairie lay golden-green and endless as a sea. No buildings could be seen, with the exception of our own barns and sleeping shed. . . . Not a tree, not a bush grew there—only wheat and grass, wheat and grass, as far as the eye could see. Nor were there any flowers. . . . No birds flew overhead; there was no movement except the swaying of the wheat in the wind; no sound but the eternal chirrup of a million grasshoppers, singing the prairie's only song.
>     We would almost collapse from the heat. When the chuck wagon came out to us at noon, we would lie on our bellies under the wagon or the horses, in order to have a bit of shade while we gobbled our food.

The attractions of the New World became a constant source of discussion in Norway, where almost everyone had a friend or relative who had emigrated. Europe's

*The age of the oceangoing steamer allowed thousands of emigrants to make a safe journey to New York or Quebec from Bergen, Oslo, or Stavanger.*

cities were plastered with advertisements about America, and most western states supported their own immigration bureau. Colorado boasted that "the young should come here to get an early start on the road to wealth."

Immigrants and native-born Americans responded fervently to such entreaties, claiming the land and extracting food from it to feed the burgeoning cities. It all happened so fast, in the few decades after train tracks spanned the continent in 1869, that it took some by surprise. In 1896, Frederick Jackson Turner, a noted historian, proclaimed that the frontier was closed, and that Manifest Destiny (the theory that the United States was destined to expand to the borders of North America) had run its course to the coasts and most points in between. Many people believed that democracy, refreshed through continuous contact with the frontier, would be weakened now that the cities, viewed as hotbeds of immorality ruled by corrupt politicians, loomed as the focal point of American life and ideals. Turner correctly saw that the vast virgin territory had been explored. But it had not all been settled. In fact, more new land was broken after 1896 than before.

*(continued on page 73)*

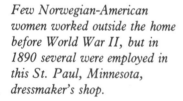

*Few Norwegian-American women worked outside the home before World War II, but in 1890 several were employed in this St. Paul, Minnesota, dressmaker's shop.*

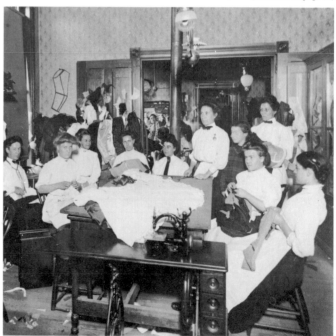

64

# CELEBRATING THE HERITAGE

Syttende Mai (*May 17th*) *parade, Brooklyn, New York, 1987. The parades are held in many American cities and towns to commemorate Norway's 1814 constitution as well as Norse influence in America.*

*Norway's seafaring history is kept alive in spirit and in fact by Norwegians in the United States and Canada. Above: The* Hjemkomst (Homecoming), *modeled on a Viking ship of the type Leif Eriksson sailed to North America around the year 1000, was built in Minnesota; in 1982 it sailed to Norway, en route docking in New York City.*

*Norwegian Americans have distinguished themselves in diverse ways. The legacy of sailing, the tradition of fine choral music in church and secular settings, and the community-minded efforts of three generations all help to bolster ethnic pride.*

*Although they rank among the most successfully assimilated groups in the United States, Norwegian Americans have held fast to their ancestral identity. Today, their aid to new immigrants from Norway strengthens the community's bonds.*

(continued from page 64)

The steady prosperity of the years under Presidents Theodore Roosevelt (1901–09) and William Howard Taft (1909–13) created a new wave of Norwegian immigration, adding another 225,000 Norwegians to the growing total. Most were farmers, but a considerable number of engineers and technicians, trained in Norway's fine schools, made the trip.

## Religion in the New Land

The first Norwegian immigrants, mainly non-Lutherans, had no financial or moral backing from organizations at home, but by the beginning of the 19th century every county in the Midwest needed a Lutheran church to satisfy the religious yearnings of the new immigrant wave. The Lutheran church in Norway initially opposed immigration, but by 1840 it began to send ministers to Wisconsin, realizing that it could not prevent the exodus. The battle between high- and low-church theology that divided Norway resurfaced on the American scene. Many settlers thought services should be more democratic, tailored to the New World, whereas others clung to the stricter, hierarchical ordering of the liturgy.

This diversity of beliefs emerged in the six Lutheran church synods that functioned simultaneously in America and Canada. Confusion reigned until 1917, when the 3 largest merged into the Norwegian Lutheran Church of America, which included Swedes and Danes among its 500,000 members but remained separate from German Lutherans. In 1946 the institution changed its name to the Evangelical Lutheran Church, and finally, in 1987, the assimilation became complete: A new association of 5.3 million members from German and Scandinavian backgrounds across the country organized themselves as the Evangelical Lutheran Church in America, the fourth-largest Protestant denomination in the country. The only sect that still remains outside the new orbit is the highly conservative, German-dominated Missouri Synod, which does not ordain women.

As Norwegian Americans scattered from coast to coast, they began to move away from their European roots and to take on American characteristics. The observations of Bjørnstjerne Bjørnson, author of Norway's national anthem and a leading Norwegian novelist, illustrate these changing beliefs and values. A spellbinding orator, Bjørnson visited America to give a lecture tour in 1881. He began in Boston, where he stayed with Ole Bull's widow. He soon met American novelist William Dean Howells, former president Ulysses S. Grant, essayist Ralph Waldo Emerson, and other national leaders. He took delight in seeing the Brooklyn Bridge being built over the East River in New York City, and he visited a large gun factory owned by two Norwegian Americans in Worcester, Massachusetts, then the nation's largest industrial city.

When Bjørnson got to the Midwest, his impressions changed. A streak of puritanism and social conservatism ran through many of those who farmed the region, and when Bjørnson said he doubted Christ's divinity, the audience reacted aggressively. Throughout the Midwest he was heckled by crowds and excoriated by Norwegian Americans who sent outraged letters to the editors of local newspapers. "Believe me, they are pretty crude, these Norwegians in Chicago," Bjørnson commented. He urged local churchmen "to heed the

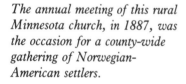

*The annual meeting of this rural Minnesota church, in 1887, was the occasion for a county-wide gathering of Norwegian-American settlers.*

dictates of culture and intellect," but to pious Norwegian Americans such words sounded like heresy. Snowbound in Iowa for 12 days during a harsh winter, Bjørnson wrote letters to his wife expressing his disbelief at the rigid thinking of the people of the farm belt.

Bjørnson hit upon one of the most salient features of American thinking, both religious and otherwise, in one observation he made during his stay: "Interiors of the churches here are often built like theaters," he wrote. "They are built according to need and not according to tradition." This design, this new thinking, he called the "fundamental difference between American and European life and institutions."

Because the boom years of Norwegian immigration to America came at a time when the first generation of settlers had already altered the physical and cultural landscape, the second generation had abandoned the idea of reestablishing the old Norway in the New World. At the beginning of the 20th century, Norway's population of 2.2 million people compared with the Norwegian population in America and Canada of nearly 1 million. It is no wonder that Bjørnson found his former countrymen to be a new breed. ✎

*Bjørnstjerne Bjørnson, who won the Nobel Prize for literature in 1903, visited Norwegian communities in America and was shocked by how quickly his former countrymen had changed.*

*Descendants of the first Norwegian immigrants pose in 1925 in front of a model of the sloop* Restauration, *which brought their ancestors to America in 1825.*

# CHANGING ALLEGIANCES

As the 20th century unfolded, Norwegian Americans, who had successfully conquered the frontier, discovered that they had to sort out their obligations to two different cultures. They often followed the path of compromise, because most members of the group wanted to fit into the New World without giving up their deeply held Norwegian traditions. Yet three important events of the early 20th century helped move Norwegian American loyalties toward America and marked the beginning of assimilation for the group as a whole.

In 1905 Norway became an independent kingdom and sovereign state for the first time in more than 500 years. Sweden's control and the dual monarchy ended diplomatically, and thousands of Norwegian Americans either sent telegrams to Oslo or journeyed there for the coronation of Haakon VII. Norway's immigrants had won their freedom the moment they landed in America, though, and this realization caused some to believe that their loyalty to the old kingdom had ended at New York harbor.

The foreign-language press in America came under attack during and after World War I. Its supporters claimed such papers were the immigrants' "only bridge" to a new society.

Although all three Scandinavian countries took a neutral stance upon the outbreak of World War I in 1914 (the centennial of Norway's constitution), suspicion arose that Norway was aiding Germany, a serious charge. Immigration to North America slowed greatly and lessened further in 1917 when the United States entered the war. The diplomatic pressure on Norway increased because the country depended on American grain shipments. In addition, Americans and Canadians of all national backgrounds felt compelled to prove their allegiance to their adopted homelands, if not by carrying a gun then at least by speaking English and boycotting German-American shops like everyone else.

Eight years later, the 100th anniversary of the landing of the *Restauration* proved equally influential. The celebrations of 1925 lasted all summer and included a speech by President Calvin Coolidge to 100,000 people in St. Paul, Minnesota; the issuing of a commemorative coin, a 5-cent stamp bearing a picture of that first schooner, and a 2-cent stamp of a Viking longboat; and a general feeling that America was glad to have 1 million Norwegians in its midst.

## Stemming the Tide

But some groups of native-born Americans had developed a severe phobia of foreigners during World War I. Immigration quotas instituted in 1921 became more strict in 1924, and even stricter still in 1927. The new quotas allowed only 2,400 new Norwegian immigrants per year with preference going to those who had family or business connections already here. The tide of immigration was stemmed.

Bigotry haunted every group of immigrants, from Greek-American bakers to Irish-Canadian teachers and Norwegian-American shopkeepers. President Woodrow Wilson, who had been a political scientist at Princeton University, said in his *History of the American People* that "some Americans need hyphens in their name because only part of them has come over." This statement, issued as America fought in Europe, sent forth an ominous message: Either bring *all* of yourself to America or go back. Theodore Roosevelt put the matter more bluntly: "The hyphen is incompatible with patriotism."

The identity conflict affected established institutions, as church and civic leaders questioned whether their goals were too ethnic. The Norwegian-Danish Conference of Methodists even considered dissolving itself as an act of patriotism. Services at Norwegian Lutheran churches began losing their native sound: In 1917, 75 percent of the services were conducted in Norwegian; by 1925 only half used Norwegian; and by 1928 the proportion dropped to 40 percent. Public and private schools alike reduced foreign-language instruction during and after the war, while newspapers printed in the mother tongue of recent immigrants either switched to English or folded.

Flagrant hostility against Norwegian Americans was rare, but to some members of the group the old country began to look more hospitable. After 1890, when one of the periodic bouts of nativism—anti-foreign attitudes—in America reared its head, the percentage of Norwegian immigrants who went back across the Atlantic increased each year. Those who returned usually were in America only a short while and did not establish deep roots.

An interesting case study of how Norwegians retained their identity can be found in Brooklyn, New York City's most populous and ethnically mixed borough. Between 1870 and 1920 the center of the Norwegian community there shifted only about six miles south, coming to rest in the Bay Ridge section overlooking New York harbor, where many Norwegian Americans worked on boats and at the docks. According to a study conducted in 1947, the 50,000 Norwegians in Brooklyn remained a tightly knit community

Rosemaling, *the painting of household items with roses, is a time-honored art practiced by Norwegian Americans.*

even as their core moved southward and several other ethnic groups settled in their midst. Through four successive moves the great majority followed along, with only a few remaining in the old section. Since the 1947 study many of the docks have closed, and a freeway now straddles Bay Ridge. Like other ethnics, those of Norwegian descent dispersed around the city and to the suburbs, but Bay Ridge continues to be the axis of Norwegian-American activity on the East Coast, and the Nordic community lives there harmoniously along with Asians, Italians, and Jews.

Though somewhat less concentrated now, the Norwegian-American community has preserved its cultural traditions through events such as the annual Syttende Mai (May 17) parade. For the celebration women wear hand-embroidered skirts and bodices, lace aprons, and a brooch of filigree, while men in shorts and red caps may do a *halling* dance. For the parade or other events, Norwegian singing clubs still perform with occasional accompaniment from a *hardingfele* (fiddle with mother-of-pearl inlay), a *langeleik* (zither), or, if someone is feeling rambunctious, a *lur* (alpenhorn) from the mountains. Perhaps the best-loved practice of artistry in the Norwegian-American community is *rosemaling* (rose painting), in which families paint ceremonial red roses on chairs, trunks, and buildings, a tradition in Norway since the 18th century. Today homes of many Norwegian Americans contain knickknacks and furnishings adorned with rosemaling.

## Choosing Their Words

During World War I, language became a political issue for American immigrants, but long before that crisis, the larger problem of official language, Riksmäl, versus common parlance Nynorsk, followed Norwegian newcomers to America. At first, Norwegian Americans used Dano-Norwegian spellings, but around 1890, common parlance took the upper hand. The simultaneous shift to English compounded the confusion, sometimes in amusing ways. The following list gives examples of how Norwegians pronounced and tried to spell some additions to their American lexicon.

| | |
|---|---|
| *blaekbor* | (blackboard) |
| *fektri* | (factory) |
| *bufflo* | (buffalo) |
| *stiffket* | (certificate) |
| *spraisparti* | (surprise party) |
| *hosspaur* | (horsepower) |
| *reit evé* | (right away) |
| *purus* | (poorhouse) |
| *lakris* | (licorice) |
| *krésé* | (crazy) |

Linguists took great delight in trying to record the conversation between, for example, a Norwegian customer and a German shopkeeper in a typical midwestern town, as the two wrestled with three languages until one word lit up four eyes in recognition. According to one scholar of the era, the American-Norwegian dialect differed so much from the European version that it proved unintelligible to new arrivals from Norway.

Nonetheless, Norwegian dialects have enriched the English language. Words describing Norwegian cuisine, such as *smorgasbord*, and *lutefisk* (codfish soaked in lye), have filtered into English, along with other words, including *fjord* and *maelstrom*. And the highlight of many Christmas gatherings and social-club lunches may be the final toast with *aquavit*, a strong, clear liquor flavored with caraway seed, a tradition in Scandinavia for hundreds of years.

Family names presented a formidable problem for many Norwegian Americans. In Norway, a child's surname can be created from the father's first name. If Ole Peterson had a son, the boy might be named Peter Olson (son of Ole). *His* son could then be named, and often was, Ole Peterson—Ole for the grandfather, and son of Peter. The repetition of names within a family and the proliferation of a few names such as Olson, Johnson, and Anderson became burdensome after a point; in the Civil War the Norwegian regiment from Wisconsin had 128 men named Ole Olson. Many Norwegians, forewarned of the confusion or else ordered to by immigration officials, took the name of their town as a surname. As a result there are many people named Bergen, or Christian (Oslo's original name), though still many more continue to call themselves Johnson or Erikson.

The large family, an American trait in the years before World War II, had been a necessity in Norway as well, and the Norwegians did not at first alter this custom when they came to the New World. Before machine power had reached the countryside, a married couple needed many children to help with house and farm work; families of 6 to 10 children were common. This pattern can still be seen today in the world's less developed countries, because in a society without social security benefits or pensions, people must rely on their children to support them in old age. The best assurance of this, in the days of high infant mortality rates, was to have as many children as possible. In America in the

*The high literacy rate among Norwegians in North America is partly the result of family reading hours.*

19th and early 20th centuries, this thinking prevailed to a large degree, especially among farm families, where more hands meant more income.

Gradually this pattern changed, for several reasons. Mechanization reduced the need for manual labor; the government began to provide pension benefits and unemployment insurance; and advances in birth control afforded couples a chance to plan the size of their family. Also, as more people moved to the cities, crowded households became less manageable.

## Typical Norwegians

Despite these changes, Norwegian Americans continued to be less urbanized than any other group, well into the 20th century. In 1948 the *Saturday Evening Post* ran a series on typical American families, choosing the Norwegian-American Offerdahls of Stoughton, Wisconsin, to illustrate farm life. Their story provides a good picture of the evolution of one town as well as of a family.

One of the Offerdahls' ancestors came to Stoughton in the 1860s, working first as a wheat farmer on land previously owned by a wealthy Yankee politician, and then in a wagon factory. He told his grandchildren that there were so many Norwegians in Stoughton that on market day lutefisk was stacked like wood outside the general store. The factory went broke during the depression, and the town suffered one of the worst unemployment rates in the state. By that time, though, the Offerdahls and their 8 children, who had bought their land at the price of $200 per acre after World War I, had several hundred acres on which they produced burley tobacco (for snuff and chaw), with corn and clover rotated in the fields to restore nitrogen to the soil. They also produced 500 gallons of milk and 100 eggs daily. Sixty hogs, a windmill, animal barns, and tobacco sheds filled out the rest of the landscape. When spare parts for the equipment were scarce during

World War II, the family members became makeshift mechanics.

Things changed after World War II. Mrs. Offerdahl remained active in the *Kvindeforening*, the aid society of the church, but there was no parade on Syttende Mai, as children of Norwegian immigrants moved on. Still, evidence of this family's ancestry could be found around the house, in the rosemaling painted on trays and wagons and walls, and in a violin made by a Norwegian from Madison, 12 miles away. Today Stoughton has yielded some of its open spaces to the approaching sprawl of Madison, and to a real-estate development for commuters. The family farms have mostly been bought up by large combines, though dairying continues to be Wisconsin's top industry and remains feasible for some small farmers. The Syttende Mai parade has been revived and is going strong again.

Norwegian immigration, reduced to a comparatively insignificant number by the 1927 quotas, suffered still more during the 1930s. The depression brought economic opportunity to a standstill, and, in fact, more people returned *to* Norway in those years than emigrated from it. Those who had hoped that ethnic identity and a vibrant, separate culture could reassert themselves after World War I were sorely disappointed. Making the world "safe for democracy," as President Woodrow Wilson put it, had to take precedence over bygone ideals. Only those who could afford to travel to Norway in search of their roots still learned Norwegian as a second language. Even St. Olaf College in Northfield, Minnesota, home of the Norwegian American Historical Association and its many publications, dropped the Norwegian-language requirement in 1921.

Ties to Norway persisted through the letters exchanged by friends and relatives, though these no longer tempted tens of thousands of emigrants each year. Norwegian Americans remembered their ancestors during the dual celebration of the 1925 centennial of the *Restauration*'s arrival in the New World, and a

*Edvard Munch, Norway's greatest artist, often portrayed modern humanity's loneliness and fear. Immigrants settling the prairie could feel similarly cut off from the world.*

statue of Abraham Lincoln was erected in Frogner Park, Oslo. A mutual insurance group, Sons of Norway, kept business and travel flowing, and the many *bygdelag* (associations of people from the same region) in America commemorated the home districts and valleys from where their parents and grandparents had come. But culturally the two nations drifted apart.

By 1914 Norway's preeminent artists and thinkers meant little to the majority of Norwegian Americans. Edvard Grieg (1843–1907) composed music that captured Norway's spirit marvelously in its rhythmic and melodic patterns—the sound of the ocean rushing upon the coast is almost palpable in his *Norwegian Concerto*—but Norwegian Americans were more devoted to church music. Edvard Munch's (1863–1944) expressionist paintings, most notably *The Scream*, evoked the tormented inner state of the lone soul in modern society at a time when the world was reluctant to give up realist and nature-oriented art.

Likewise, Henrik Ibsen (1828–1906), the father of modern drama and arguably the greatest creative mind Norway ever produced, did not receive nationwide approval in America. When *A Doll's House* (1879) had its American premiere in Milwaukee in 1882, Americans attacked its bold assertion of women's rights. A Chicago reviewer called it a masterpiece, but claimed the "Godless life" it described would lead to the "dissolution of the bond of every relationship." In the Norwegian-American press the play's reception ran from cool to vicious.

Coming on the heels of Bjørnstjerne Bjørnson's calamitous visit the year before, Ibsen's ideas met with similar disapproval on the frontier. Norwegian Americans, mainly preoccupied with starting life anew, relied upon the sacred values of church, home, and family they had transplanted from the Old World.

In many ways the Norwegians who came to North America were lucky. They came at a time when land was cheap and available; they came from a country with a good educational system that provided useful training for building cities and farms; and they did not suffer the extreme prejudice that left millions of less fortunate immigrants barred from jobs, excluded from clubs, or locked out of neighborhoods because of the color of their skin or their religious beliefs. On the other hand, the Norwegians suffered the cruel hand of nature more than most, experiencing the cold of the inhospitable North and the hunger, insect plagues, loneliness, sickness, and taxing manual labor of rural life.

Generally, Norwegians kept up their contact with Europe more diligently than others in the Midwest, in some cases staying spiritually closer to it than immigrants on the East Coast, despite living geographically farther away. Isolated on farms, Norwegians may have needed the moral support provided by contact with the old country. Those back home in Norway, eager for land and opportunity, encouraged this contact, pressing their overseas kin for letters.

Norwegian Americans left their mark on the land itself as much as on other people, most often on dry, flat plains unlike anything they had ever seen. Today, those who come to Brooklyn or Seattle find a city in some ways similar to Oslo, mostly because of inherent likenesses between any two industrialized 20th-century cities. More importantly, immigrants today arrive better informed about their new home, and have a more prosperous and established community to greet them.

*This carved-wood altarpiece, fashioned by an immigrant, now belongs to the Norwegian-American Museum at Vesterheim, Iowa.*

*Gro Svendsen came to Iowa in 1862 at age 21. Her letters chronicle the resilience of strangers in a rugged land.*

# Making a Name in America

Though people of Norwegian descent have never composed more than two percent of America's total population, they have made an impact in many fields. They have shown a bent for church life, science, engineering, and government (in 1925 the United States had 4 governors and 15 congressmen of Norwegian ancestry). Norwegian Americans have also succeeded as athletes, entertainers, businesspeople, and artists.

Most prominent Norwegian Americans have been men, and for an obvious reason. Until World War II, women seldom had an opportunity to pursue careers outside the home. Nonetheless, some women made their mark. One was Gro Svendsen, frontier farmer and mother. Svendsen came to Iowa from Hallingdal in 1862, at age 21, and bore 10 children before her death (in childbirth) at age 37. She managed to find enough free moments in her routine, however, to write numerous letters to her loved ones in Norway. This correspondence described her experiences in America and has been collected and published in a book, *Frontier Mother*.

In a typical letter, Svendsen reported on the Atlantic crossing: "The cold waves break against the decks, and the timbers creak in the sloop. The furniture moves about as if possessed." On board, sailors ogled and pestered her, and she glimpsed the first black person she had ever seen. Later, America defeated all expectations. "It is so vastly different from Norway," she commented in one letter, " . . . and also quite different from what we imagined it was when we were at home—when one thought only of the benefits and comforts and forgot the other side of the venture." A natural writer, Svendsen filled her correspondence with striking details of farm life, describing muskmelons "big as a child's head" and explaining how maggots are kept off butter with salt and brine. In June, "the locusts came like a blinding drift of snow. When they fly, they seem to be all white, but down on the Earth they are brown. They settled down on the wheat, . . . on each straw, and they began their devastating feast." In addition to writing home, Svendsen contributed articles to the newspaper *Emigranten*, hauled wood six miles, got bitten by fleas, washed clothes with lye, and nursed infants. For all her energy, she found it "disturbing" that Americans worked on the Sabbath, one law of the frontier she refused to abide.

Loneliness emerges as the saddest theme of Svendsen's letters. She missed Norway terribly, mentioning in one letter that "my love for my native land is far too deep and far too sacred. I could never prefer any other country to my own." Her sorrow worsened when her husband Ole left for the Civil War and when some of her babies died. When Gro Svendsen died, Ole moved the family away, but not before planting a tree on her grave to keep off weeds. He wrote to her parents, "I . . . send you a lock of my dear Gro's hair. . . . How much I miss her cannot be told." Svendsen's life, mingling loss with happiness, exemplified the fortitude of millions of immigrant women.

A later Norwegian American, Earl Warren, pioneered a different frontier. The son of a Norwegian father, whose original name was Varren, and a Swedish mother, Warren himself was born in Los Angeles in 1891. He began his political career as a hardfighting attorney general in California in the 1930s; his reputation reached national proportions with his election as governor of California in 1942, an office he held for three terms. As the state's chief executive, Warren increased pensions for the elderly, lowered the sales tax, bolstered unemployment insurance, and beefed up the state's child-care programs. In 1948, he lost a bid for the vice-presidency, running on the ticket with Republican presidential candidate Thomas Dewey. In 1953, however, President Eisenhower named Warren the new chief justice of the United States Supreme Court. He served in that position until 1969, and died in 1974.

A longtime Republican, Warren startled the nation—and the president who appointed him—by taking controversial stances on major constitutional issues. A year after his induction, Warren ruled, in *Brown v. the Board of Education*, that segregation could no longer be allowed in America's public schools. This decision reversed a 50-year-old ruling, *Plessy v. Ferguson*, which deemed that "separate but equal" facilities for blacks were consistent with the 14th Amendment's guarantee of full rights for all citizens. In subsequent cases the same principle stated in *Brown* was used to end segregation in interstate commerce, bus terminals and airports, parks, and virtually all public buildings. These important decisions helped spark the civil rights movement that continues today.

Warren's humane views emerged in other issues related to civil rights. He led the Supreme Court in restricting the government's ability to conduct investigations such as those instigated by Senator Joseph McCarthy in the 1950s and also in restricting the power of the FBI to withhold information from people it prosecuted. Earl Warren, by setting the tone for the court he presided over, came to represent the foremost ideals of American civil liberties, and he holds a high place in history.

*Earl Warren, the son of Norwegian and Swedish parents, served as chief justice of the United States from 1953 to 1969, and helped usher in the civil rights era.*

Another Norwegian-American politician, Hubert H. Humphrey, began his career as a liberal and remained one until his death. Born above a drugstore in Canton, South Dakota, in 1911, he graduated from the University of Minnesota in 1939 and received a master of arts in political philosophy from Louisiana State University, then taught at several academic institutions, including Macalester College in St. Paul, Minnesota. At the same time, he entered politics, leading the Minnesota campaign to reelect President Franklin D. Roosevelt in 1944. The next year, Humphrey became mayor of Minneapolis; in 1948 he won election to the U.S. Senate and won again in 1954 and 1960. Four years later the Democratic party chose him as its vice-presidential candidate on a ticket headed by Lyndon Baines Johnson. They swept to victory and seemed poised to run in 1968 when Johnson suddenly announced his retirement from politics. Humphrey then became the party's presidential nominee. Unable to distance himself from Johnson's controversial handling of the Vietnam War, Humphrey failed to unite the party and lost the election to Republican Richard Nixon by less than one percent of the popular vote.

In 1970 Humphrey reentered the Senate, then won reelection in 1976. He died in 1978. Throughout his long career, Humphrey remained steadfast in support-

*As mayor, senator, and vice-president, Hubert Humphrey usually spoke for workers, the elderly, and the disadvantaged. He narrowly lost the 1968 presidential election to Richard M. Nixon.*

ing greater federal action, particularly in helping the less privileged. He fought for labor and against corporations; he spoke out for old-age medical insurance and civil rights long before other congressmen came around to these views. As a senator he worked for arms control and a nuclear test-ban treaty with the Soviet Union. He proved his adeptness as a party politician by ousting communists from the Democratic Party in 1947. Humphrey's legacy encapsulates the decades of work by hundreds of like-minded Norwegian Americans who also fought for better social legislation.

## The Great and the Gifted

Although government attracted some Norwegian Americans, others aided their adopted homeland in less public ways. Scientist Ernest O. Lawrence never became a household name, but his work proved revolutionary. Lawrence's Norwegian parents immigrated to South Dakota, where his father eventually became superintendent of schools. Ernest Lawrence studied at St. Olaf College in Northfield, Minnesota, the University of South Dakota, and Yale University. At the age of 29 he became a full professor of physics at the University of Chicago. In 1929 he conceived the idea of smashing the atom, and then designed and built the first cyclotron to do it. With his brother John, a doctor, he devised a way to put the cyclotron's neutron rays to work killing cancerous tumors in humans without exposing them to radiation. In 1938, when Lawrence won the Nobel Prize for physics, he turned over his prize money to the University of California so that a bigger cyclotron could be built. Lawrence later discovered the key isotope uranium-238—a crucial element of the atomic bomb—and became 1 of 6 scientists named to manage the Manhattan Project, charged with developing the atomic bomb during World War II.

Lawrence's genius had a lighthearted side. He answered his children's curiosity about television by building a set in his garage, later demonstrating how it

The son of Norwegian immigrants, Ernest Lawrence became one of the leading scientists of his time. He invented the cyclotron to smash atoms and conducted experiments in the medical uses of radiation.

*Ole Evinrude developed the outboard motor that bears his name.*

*Ole Evinrude developed the outboard motor that bears his name.*

worked to curious government officials. When his colleagues joked that he could turn mercury to gold like a magician he recalled his native state and replied that it was "much easier to go out in the hills and dig for it."

Another Norwegian-born inventor, Ole Evinrude, designed and built the first outboard motor in 1907. He got the idea while rowing across a Wisconsin lake, carrying ice cream to his girlfriend. Ole Singstad, chief engineer of the Holland Tunnel, which connects New York City and New Jersey by running underneath the Hudson River, helped develop the ventilation and roadways used for underwater tunnels from 1920–27. The same model has been used for all tunnels since.

In sports, one Norwegian American, Babe Didrikson, stands above all. Born in 1914 in Texas to immigrants, she became, in the words of sportswriter Grantland Rice, "the athletic phenomenon of all time, man or woman." Babe, nicknamed for Babe Ruth, won gold medals at the 1932 Olympics in the javelin and hurdles, and also surpassed all her competitors in the high jump, though she placed second because of a technicality. She excelled at tennis, basketball, and skating, before taking up golf as a professional. Babe then proceeded to win 56 golf tournaments, creating an enormous following of supporters. Didrikson, who married wrestler George Zaharias, demonstrated single-handedly that women superstars can be as exciting as their male counterparts.

*Once called "the athletic phenomenon of all time," Babe Didrikson Zaharias excelled at many sports. In her later years, she dominated the women's professional golf circuit.*

Knute Rockne, a high-school dropout in Chicago but an "A" student in chemistry at Notre Dame in 1914, achieved national renown as that university's football coach. Rockne transformed the Fighting Irish into the greatest power in the game, leading them to five perfect seasons. He also revolutionized the sport by introducing intricate offensive alignments that featured star combinations such as "the Four Horsemen," the best-known backfield in football history. An inspiring coach, in one of his halftime speeches Rockne exhorted his team to "win one for the Gipper," a phrase now known to almost all Americans.

## Further Achievements

Immigrants sometimes faced opposition in the business world, hampered by their imperfect English or by prejudice. The second generation faced fewer obstacles. The ranks of successful Norwegian-American business-

*Football coach Knute Rockne, born in Norway, made his mark on American sport by popularizing the forward pass at Notre Dame University.*

men include Arthur Andersen, founder of the world's largest accounting firm, which bears his name. Orphaned as a child in Illinois, he went on to head the accounting department at Northwestern University at an early age. In later years, congressional committees frequently asked Andersen to contribute his vast knowledge to their investigations. Another Norwegian-American businessman, James Olson, spent his entire career as a technician and manager for Bell Telephone, and from 1986 to 1988 he was chairman of AT&T, the world's largest communications company.

Thorstein Veblen (1857–1929), born into a Wisconsin immigrant family, towered over American economic and sociological thinking during the first decades of the 20th century. His classic *The Theory of the Leisure Class* criticized and satirized American economic practices. The term *conspicuous consumption*, coined by Veblen, is still used in discussions of wasteful materialism. *The Theory of the Leisure Class* won a large following among those who argued for dismantling large corporations and placing some of the nation's wealth in the hands of the laborers who actually produced it. Veblen's book also influenced New Deal strategists who sought to rescue America's devastated economy in the 1930s. Veblen's other books underscored the theme that if business finance could be as rationally arranged as industrial production, most waste might be eliminated.

*The writings of social critic and economist Thorstein Veblen influenced government and business practice from 1900 through the 1930s.*

## From a Different Viewpoint

The most penetrating analyses of society do not always come from philosophers and political scientists. Storytellers also provide insight into the way we live by focusing on details that go unobserved by scholarly writers. Two fiction writers of Norwegian descent, Ole Rölvaag and Garrison Keillor, have offered their gifts and insights to fashion stories well known to thousands of readers.

Ole Edvart Rölvaag, born in 1876, grew up on Dönna, a small, treeless island off Norway's coast and just south of the Arctic Circle. At 15 Rölvaag joined fishing crews that sailed on daylong expeditions. In the winter, the Dönnans ate only potatoes and salt herring at each meal, feeding their cattle with dried kelp picked from the rocks. At 20 Rölvaag turned down the chance to run his own fishing boat and accepted his uncle's offer to join him on his farm in South Dakota. Rölvaag landed in New York in 1896 with a dime and a Norwegian copper in his pocket. He spent the dime on tobacco and ate just one loaf of bread during the three-day train ride west. No one met him at the station, so he walked half the night until he found someone who spoke Norwegian and directed him to the farm. Rölvaag stayed with his uncle for three years.

Soon, however, Rölvaag developed an interest in fiction and wrote *Giants in the Earth*, America's most celebrated chronicle of pioneer experience and Norwegian life. It has stayed popular since its English translation in 1924. A review in *The Nation*, an influential journal, called it the "most powerful novel that has been written about pioneer life in America."

The novel traces the experience of Per Hansa, who in 1866 leaves Minnesota with his wife Beret and their three children and arrives in the Dakota Territory. As the homesteaders start life anew, they break the land, lose cattle, attempt to time their planting and harvesting, and most dispiriting of all, they try to combat the loneliness of existence so far from the known world. Beret Hansa, especially, suffers from isolation, struggling to perform her lonely household chores while the men toil together in the field. Beret becomes a powerless witness as locust plagues, poor crop years, blizzards, and bad luck all strike her family, leading her to believe that some evil force rules their lives. She loses the capacity to enjoy even simple pleasures and retreats into the Bible and her memories of a happy childhood. A minister passes through town, and at Per Hansa's urging he convinces Beret that Satan does not inhabit her soul. Yet even after hearing these consoling words,

## GIANTS IN THE EARTH
### By O. E. RÖLVAAG

*The* fullest, finest and most powerful novel that has been written about pioneer life in America

BURT

75¢

FICTION

Beret's face "carried the same childlike expression . . . her eyes had the same dreamy, far-away stare; they seemed to be seeing something she did not want to behold, looking for something that would never happen; hence the strange sadness that always shone through them." The book's final chapter, called "The Great Plain Drinks the Blood of Christian Men and Is Satisfied," sums up how minuscule their efforts have been.

Nonetheless, the Hansas make a success of their newly chosen life. The book's title refers to trolls and spirits who, according to Norse mythology, lurk within the land, looming in Norway's mountains and rugged terrain and, in a more malevolent form, populate the Kingdom of Darkness and Evil that lies underground to the north. But the title takes on another meaning for the Hansas and their fellow pioneers in the West. The giants are the settlers themselves, conquering the land

*In his novel* Giants in the Earth, *Ole Rölvaag fused his perceptions about the Norwegian temperament with his firsthand knowledge of the hardships of breaking new land.*

*Humor with a small-town twist has received a boost from best-selling author Garrison Keillor, creator of the mythical town of Lake Wobegon.*

with their hands, shaping the earth into accordance with the human will to survive:

> Such soil! Only to sink the plow in it, to turn over the sod—and there was a field ready for seeding . . . it was soil for *wheat*, the king of all grains! Such soil had been created by the good Lord to bear this noble seed; and here was Per Hansa, walking around on a hundred and sixty acres of it, all his very own!

Rölvaag wrote two sequels to *Giants*, one concerning the Hansa boy born in a sod hut, *Peder Victorious*. At that book's end, as one scholar put it, Per Hansa decided to "let Peder become what America makes him."

A more recent Norwegian-American writer and humorist, Garrison Keillor focuses not on the prairie, but on small-town life. Keillor's first book, a collection of short stories called *Happy to Be Here* (1982), gives a comical account of humble folks in the Midwest. In his second book, *Lake Wobegon Days* (1985), Keillor focuses on the town of Lake Wobegon, Minnesota, and its few hundred descendants of Norwegian Lutherans and German Catholics. He had previously created the town and people of Lake Wobegon on his weekly radio program, "A Prairie Home Companion," which included folk music, storytelling, and fake commercials. The show ended in June 1987 after 13 years on the air, and its stories about the Wobegonians were collected in yet another best-selling book, *Leaving Home* (1987). Keillor's nostalgic method plays well alongside his dry humor and compassion. Humor that scoffs at small-town values and institutions (church suppers, gossip, the imperviousness to change) has always been an American staple, but Keillor has turned mockery aside in favor of more universal jokes with a strong element of sympathy and nostalgia. The citizens of Lake Wobegon talk slowly, "drop words a few at a time like beans on a hill," and live in "the little town that time forgot."

Like most real small towns today, Lake Wobegon maintains a solid population of older people, such as Hjalmar Ingqvist:

Homesickness hit the old-timers hard, even after so many years, and it was not unusual to see old people weep openly for Norway or hear about old men so sad they took a bottle of whiskey up to the cemetery and lay down on the family grave and talked to the dead about home, the home in Norway, heavenly Norway. America was the land where they were old and sick, Norway where they were young and full of hopes and much smarter, for you are never so smart again in a language learned in middle age nor so romantic or brave or kind. All the best of you is in the old tongue, but when you speak your best in America you become a yokel, a dumb Norskie, and when you speak English, an idiot. No wonder the old-timers loved the places where the mother tongue was spoken, the Evangelical Lutheran church, the Sons of Knute lodge, the tavern.

Keillor's popularity may be evidence that America, for all of its modern, urban sophistication, still lingers over memories of its small-town history. Even the radio-show format paid tribute to the flavor of small towns and bygone days. Much of Keillor's material about preachers, old ladies, dogs, ball games, the Main Street tavern, and the like, is ripe with nostalgia for a disappearing way of life, yet the listener or reader is always aware that an element of old-fashioned simplicity is part of his own character, too, no matter where he lives.

Keillor himself grew up in the town of Anoka, Minnesota, in the 1950s and 1960s, a third-generation Norwegian American. In 1987 he married a Danish woman, and after the radio show ended, moved to Denmark to write full-time. After a few months in Copenhagen, the couple moved to New York City. But Lake Wobegon, "where all the women are strong, the men are good-looking, and all the children are above average," is alive again in a new locale—Keillor will stage "A Prairie Home Companion" not weekly in St. Paul but once a year at New York City's Carnegie Hall. ❧

*In 1900, members of a Norwegian-American social club in Seattle display their dual allegiance by flying two flags.*

# PASSING THE TORCH

Although North America probably offers more economic opportunity than anywhere else in the world, Norwegians now arrive at a much slower rate than before 1914. Immigrants numbered about 2,000 per year during the 1950s and 1960s; in the 1970s newcomers dwindled to only a few hundred per year.

Declining immigration stems in part from the events of the 20th century. In World War II Norway was invaded and occupied by the Nazis. American president Franklin D. Roosevelt said at the time, "If there is anyone who still wonders why this war is being fought, let him look to Norway." The Norwegian government went into exile in London while its armed forces regrouped in Canada. A whole village called Little Norway grew up around the training base in Toronto, and the assistance given by Canada remains a source of goodwill between the two nations. After the war Norway's economy recovered and the country became reintegrated with the rest of Europe.

Although emigration has slowed, jet travel has increased contact between Norway and America. The Norway Cup, for instance, the world's largest youth soccer tournament, attracts dozens of teams from America and elsewhere each year. America has now begun a similar tournament to return the favor. Adding to the chances for community and cultural exchange is the ability of most modern Norwegians to speak English (it is a required subject in Norway's public schools).

## Welcoming New Arrivals

In many Norwegian-American communities, the Torske Klubben, a philanthropic and social organization of Norwegian-American men, gathers monthly for a meal of lutefisk, flatbread, and much toasting with aquavit. The club began in Minneapolis in 1933, and since 1960 eight other chapters have been started, two of them in Canada and the newest in Arizona, reflecting the group's population shift to the sun belt. One Torske Klubben sponsors graduate students from Norway for a year of study at the University of Minnesota. Fellowship winners have distinguished themselves in diverse fields such as art, forestry, engineering, business, and history. A new fellowship established in the 1980s sends American students to Norway.

The few immigrants who come to the United States from Norway today mainly settle in the group's strongholds—Brooklyn, Seattle, and Minneapolis. Life in these large cities can blur ethnic traces. At the same time, however, American cities have become more international in composition and character than ever before, and Norwegian Americans enrich the palette.

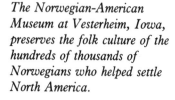

*The Norwegian-American Museum at Vesterheim, Iowa, preserves the folk culture of the hundreds of thousands of Norwegians who helped settle North America.*

Norwegian immigrants have always succeeded at fitting into North American culture. As early as the 1840s one native American made this laudatory remark, recorded by an itinerant Norwegian journalist:

> Never have I known people to become so civilized so rapidly as your countrymen; they come here in motley crowds, dressed up with all kinds of dingle-dangle just like the Indians. But just look at them a year later: they speak English perfectly, and, as far as dress, manners, and ability are concerned they are quite above reproach.

Such ready acceptance by the new hosts has always greased the wheels of assimilation for Norwegians. Acceptance has its drawbacks, however. In the 1920s, Ole Rölvaag, the Norwegian-American novelist, believed that Norwegian Americans gave evidence of "succumbing to the effects of mass suggestion, and . . . fervently denying their origin." He would be gladdened by subsequent developments within the community. In the

*The large contingent of Norwegians in and around Brooklyn, New York, celebrate their Constitution Day every year on* Syttende Mai *(May 17), as do Norwegian Americans in other cities.*

1980s, most of the 3.5 million Norwegian descendants in the United States and Canada wear their ancestry as a badge of pride.

In several cities the Syttende Mai parade provides a yearly occasion for bringing out the old stories and garb and paying tribute to Norway's constitution. The 1987 Syttende Mai parade in Brooklyn lasted two hours and included bands from three countries. Keynote speaker Theis Pedersen, consul of the Norwegian Trade Commission, urged that Canada, Norway, and the United States, along with the other western democracies, fight "for human rights and decency."

Norway remains at the forefront of nations trying to build an egalitarian society. A woman, Gro Harlem Brundtland, became the country's prime minister in 1986, and women occupy half the posts in the cabinet. The *New York Times* has commented that the advancement of women in Norwegian society "offers an attractive taste of the future." The same could be said of Norwegian Americans, whose hard work has earned them many rewards and alerted their neighbors to the great strides made by this proud ethnic group. ⮞

# FURTHER READING

Benton, Barbara. *Ellis Island: A Pictorial History*. New York: Facts on File, 1985.

Bergmann, Leola N. *Americans from Norway*. Westport, CT: Greenwood Press, 1973.

Bjork, Kenneth. *West of the Great Divide*. Northfield, MN: Norwegian-American Historical Association, 1958.

Blegen, Theodore C. *Norwegian Migration to America, 1825–1860*. New York: Arno Press, 1969.

Forbes, Kathryn. *Mama's Bank Account*. New York: Scholastic, Inc., 1975. [Fiction]

Haugen, Einar, and Eva Lund Haugen, trans. *Land of the Free: Bjornstjerne Bjornson's American Letters, 1880–1881*. Northfield, MN: Norwegian-American Historical Association, 1978.

Hillbrand, Percie V., ed. *Norwegians in America*. Minneapolis, MN: Lerner Publications, 1967.

Keillor, Garrison. *Lake Wobegon Days*. New York: Penguin Books, 1986. [Fiction]

———. *Leaving Home*. New York: Viking Press, 1987. [Fiction]

Rölvaag, Ole. *Giants in the Earth*. Trans. by Lincold Colcord. New York: Harper & Row, 1965. [Fiction]

Svendsen, Gro. *Frontier Mother: The Letters of Gro Svendsen*. Trans. by Theodore Blegen and Pauline Farseth. Northfield, MN: Norwegian-American Historical Association, 1950.

# INDEX

Aasen, Ivar, 22
Adams, John Quincy, 32
"Age of Wergeland," 26
Amundsen, Roald, 19
Andersen, Arthur, 97
Anoka, Minnesota, 101
Arctic Ocean, 17

Bay Ridge, New York, 80, 81
Beaver Creek, Illinois, 34, 41
Bergen, Hans, 31
Bergen, Norway, 17, 37, 57
Bjørnson, Bjørnstjerne, 51, 52, 74, 75, 87
"Black Death," 20
Black Hawk, Chief, 40
Bonaparte, Napoleon, 23, 24, 27
Bønder, 25, 34
Bosque County, Texas, 34
Brooklyn, New York, 15, 53, 80, 87, 104
Brown v. the Board of Education, 91
Brundtland, Gro Harlem, 106
Bull, Ole, 46

California Gold Rush, 50
Cambridge, Massachusetts, 46
Canada, 15, 29, 31, 37, 46, 47, 57, 75
Canarsee Indians, 31
Canton, South Dakota, 92
Chicago, Illinois, 15, 33, 41, 46, 53, 58, 61, 96
Civil War, the U.S., 35, 37, 40, 43, 49, 52, 60, 82, 90
Clausen, A. C., 51
Coolidge, Calvin, 78

Delaware River, 31
Denmark, 20, 21, 23, 26
Dewey, Thomas, 91
Didrikson, Babe, 94, 95
Doll's House, A (Ibsen), 86
Dönna, island of, 97
Door County, Wisconsin, 42, 43

Eisenhower, Dwight D., 91
Ellida, 37

Emerson, Ralph Waldo, 74
Erie Canal, 32
Eriksson, Leif, 19, 20
Erik the Red, 19
Evinrude, Ole, 94

Fairhair, Harald, king of Norway, 20
Finland, 17
Fox River, 33, 34, 37
Frederik, Christian, 23
Frontier Mother (Svendsen), 89

Gaspé, Quebec, 46, 47
Giants in the Earth, (Rölvaag), 98
Grant, Ulysses S., 74
Great Lakes, 15, 37
Great Northern Railroad, 45
Green Bay, Wisconsin, 42
Greenland, 31
Grieg, Edvard, 86
Gulf of St. Lawrence, 47

Haakon IV, king of Norway, 20, 73
Hamsun, Knut, 63
Happy to Be Here (Keillor), 100
Hauge, Hans Nielsen, 27
Heg, Even, 49
Heyerdahl, Thor, 19
Hill, James J., 45
History of the American People (Wilson), 79
Hofstadter, Richard, 54, 55
Holter, Anton, 57
Homestead Act of 1862, 55, 62
Honmyhr, John, 61
Howells, William Dean, 74
Hudson Bay, Canada, 20
Hudson River, 32, 33, 94
Hudson Strait, 31, 33
Humphrey, Hubert, 92, 93

Ibsen, Henrik, 86
Iceland, 31
Iverson, A. M., 42

Johnson, Lyndon Baines, 92
Juneau, Alaska, 57

Keillor, Garrison, 97, 100, 101
Kendall township, New York, 33, 34, 36
Kloster, Christopher, 47
Knutson, Steener, 44

La Crosse, Wisconsin, 44
Lake Michigan, 33, 37, 42
Lake Ontario, 33
Lake Superior, 42
*Lake Wobegon Days* (Keillor), 100
Lawrence, Ernest O., 93
*Leaving Home* (Keillor), 100
Lincoln, Abraham, 25, 52, 85
Liverpool, England, 35
London, England, 103
Los Angeles, California, 91
Luther, Martin, 22
Luther College, 45

McCarthy, Joseph, 91
Madison, Wisconsin, 43, 44, 46, 58, 85
*Mayflower*, 31
Mediterranean Sea, 19
Milwaukee, Wisconsin, 43, 49
Minneapolis, Minnesota, 58, 61, 104
Minuit, Peter, 31
Mississippi River, 34, 61
Missouri Synod, 52, 73
Moravians, 42
Munch, Edvard, 86
Muskego, Wisconsin, 43, 44, 50

Nansen, Fridtjof, 19
Napoleonic Wars, 27
Nelson, Knute, 54
New York, New York, 74, 94
Nixon, Richard M., 92
Northfield, Minnesota, 85
Norway
  constitution of, 24
  geography of, 17
  history of, 17–29
  kingdom of, 17, 24
  regional dialects of, 23
Norway Cup, the, 103

Norwegian-American Historical Association, 85
Norwegian Americans
  ancestry of, 14
  artists, 86
  cultural traditions, 81, 82
  early immigration to the United States, 32–37
  early settling in the United States, 13, 15
  loyalty to native districts, 28, 29
  newspapers, 49–51
  population figures, 14, 15, 61
  reasons for immigrating, 28, 29
  religion of, 73–75
  writers, 86, 97–101
Norwegian Canadians, 15, 37, 46, 47, 57, 75
*Norwegian Concerto* (Grieg), 86
Notre Dame University, 96

Oakland, California, 56
Oleana, Pennsylvania, 46
Olsen, Lars, 32
Olson, James, 97
Oslo, Norway, 28, 57, 85, 87
Ostenso, Martha, 57

Pedersen, Theis, 106
*Peder Victorious* (Rölvaag), 100
Peerson, Cleng, 33
*Plessy v. Ferguson*, 91
Portland, Oregon, 15
"Prairie Home Companion, A," 100, 101

Reformation, 22
Reierson, Johannes, 59
*Restauration*, 13, 32, 37, 78
Rockne, Knute, 96
Rölvaag, Ole, 97–100, 105
Roosevelt, Franklin D., 92, 103
Roosevelt, Theodore, 73, 79
Rynning, Ole, 34, 37

St. Olaf College, 85
San Francisco, California, 56
*Scream, The* (Munch), 86

Seattle, Washington, 15, 57, 87, 104
Singstad, Ole, 94
Skagerrak Strait, 21
Stavanger, Norway, 13, 17, 32, 33, 37
Steenerson, Knute, 45
Stoughton, Wisconsin, 84, 85
Sugar Creek, Iowa, 45
Svendsen, Gro, 36, 37, 87, 90
Sweden, 17, 20, 21, 23, 24, 29, 77
*Syttende Mai* (May 17), 23, 81, 85, 106

Taft, William Howard, 73
Tank, Nils Otto, 42
Telemark, Norway, 44
*Theory of the Leisure Class, The* (Veblen), 97
Thrane, Marcus, 53
Torske Klubben, 104
Trondheim, Norway, 17
*True Account of America* (Rynning), 34, 37

Trygvason, Olaf, 22

Ueland, Ole Gabriel, 25
Union of the Crowns, 23
Union of Kalmar, 21–23
University of Minnesota, 104

Vancouver, Canada, 15
Vanderbilt, Jan, 31
Veblen, Thorstein, 97
Vesterheim (museum), 46
Vikings, 19–21

Waerenskjold, Elise, 59
Warren, Earl, 90, 91
Webster, Daniel, 50
Wergeland, Henrik, 25, 26
Whitman, Walt, 26
*Wild Geese* (Ostenso), 57
Wilson, Woodrow, 79
Worcester, Massachusetts, 74
World War I, 49, 51, 78, 79
World War II, 83, 84, 93, 103

# PICTURE CREDITS

JAMES M. CORNELIUS, born in Minneapolis in 1959, is an editor living in New York City. He is a graduate of Lawrence University and has written book reviews for the *Minneapolis Tribune,* the *Cleveland Plain Dealer,* and *Publishers Weekly.*

DANIEL PATRICK MOYNIHAN is the senior United States senator from New York. He is also the only person in American history to serve in the cabinets or subcabinets of four successive presidents—Kennedy, Johnson, Nixon, and Ford. Formerly a professor of government at Harvard University, he has written and edited many books, including *Beyond the Melting Pot, Ethnicity: Theory and Experience* (both with Nathan Glazer), *Loyalties,* and *Family and Nation.*